Journals from the Ant-heap

Journals from the Ant-heap

Dannie Abse

Hutchinson
London   Melbourne   Auckland   Johannesburg

This edition first published in 1986 by Hutchinson Ltd, an imprint of
Century Hutchinson Ltd., Brookmount House, 62–65 Chandos Place,
London, WC2N 4NW

Century Hutchinson Australia (Pty) Ltd.,
PO Box 496, 16–22 Church Street, Hawthorn, Melbourne, Victoria 3122

Century Hutchinson New Zealand Limited
PO Box 40–086, 32–34 View Road, Glenfield, Auckland 10

Century Hutchinson South Africa (Pty) Ltd.
PO Box 337, Berglvei 2012, South Africa

ISBN 0 09 167321 6

Some of the material in this book was first published elsewhere. Thus
acknowledgements are owed to the *Hampstead and Highgate Express* for
'Abse's 1984'; to Cecil Woolf for 'Authors Take Sides on the Falklands';
to University College, Cardiff Press for 'Under the Influence of'; and to
the *Poetry Review* for 'The Chairman'.

I am indebted also to a number of friends, not least Tony Whittome of
Hutchinson, Cary Archard of the Poetry Wales Press, and Patricia Oxley,
editor of *Acumen*.

Printed and bound in Great Britain
The Guernsey Press Co. Ltd., Guernsey, Channel Islands.

To Margaret and Giles Gordon

INTRODUCTION

Gerald Isaaman, the editor of a local newspaper in London, the *Hampstead and Highgate Express*, affectionately known as the *Ham and High*, is a great admirer of George Orwell. In December 1983, recalling Orwell's once lively column for *Tribune* entitled 'As I Please', he decided that, during 1984, he would like a similar series to grace the pages of the *Ham and High*.

George Orwell, alas, was not available. So he cast around for other writers, shortlisting a number of them, no doubt alphabetically, for soon he telephoned me. I could not mimic Orwell. I could only write my own kind of prose. Gerald did not seem to mind and I agreed to offer him a fortnightly autobiographical column for one year only. He was to call my non-Orwellian 'As I Please' 'ABSE'S 1984'. He proved to be an ideal editor. He only very occasionally made suggestions and never changed my copy.

In March 1985 it was suggested to me that I protract my journal so that it could be published in book form. I could continue writing it, of course, as I pleased, and more importantly, when I pleased. I cannot pretend that I have not enjoyed conjugating occasional autobiographical items while I have been based in London or in South Wales. And I hope they will amuse like-minded readers. They are not private diary entries but were written, as all journalism is, as a public secret.

Abse's
1984

January 1984

Shouts from Joan half-way up the stairs. Wild shouts. Caitlin has brought a mouse into our house again.

Joan calls: 'The bloody thing's alive like last time.' Last time I had to kill the mouse. I loathed that.

Caitlin has taken her victim into the living room. Reluctantly, slow as a policeman, I investigate, hoping the cat will kill the mouse before I arrive. Caitlin is crouched threateningly and, whoops, the mouse suddenly flies a yard into the air.

It's not a mouse at all. It's a bird, an ordinary, London, Golders Green, NW11, sparrow. A commotion and the bird has flopped behind a bookcase. 'It's a bird,' I yell. Joan, in no way afraid of birds, enters the living room.

She is more comfortable with birds than I am. I could not kill a bird. We ambush Caitlin, banish her, shut the door into the hall so that the cat cannot come in, open the door into the garden so that the bird, if not damaged, can go out.

The bird is very still behind the bookcase. Has it a broken wing or leg? The packed bookcase proves too heavy to shift. Slowly, trying not to frighten the sparrow, we move the books. The bird does not move. At last we can edge the bookcase gently away from the wall. The bird is exposed.

Go, go, go, bird. There is the door, there is the cold January garden. There is freedom of a sort.

It is a long time before the bird stirs. Then it hops. Its legs are OK. It flies! It flies, it flies through the door, away! We have saved the bird. Joan is a heroine, I am a hero. We are pleased with each other, with ourselves. But all over the carpet there are feathers, here, there, so many feathers.

1984 has begun this way, like an omen.

On January 1, shouldn't those seers with hangovers – poets? – put on their purple magicians' cloaks, stare into their perspex balls and translate silence? King Hussain will be assassinated before the year's out. Someone will mount Arafat. Reagan will suffer from bowel cancer. Heseltine will make a huge fool of himself . . . again. Albania will have a new leader.

It seems, though, that when I make prophetic assertions like that I am invariably wrong.

For instance, I recall D. M. Thomas who had just been made redundant from Hereford College of Further Education, telling me gloomily: 'I'll have to write a novel, make cash that way.' I shook my head, tried to dissuade him. 'You're wasting your time, you'll never make money writing a serious novel.' I was absolutely sure I was right.

Then there was that occasion when I was a member of a local charity brains trust. The panel included the MP for Finchley, a certain Margaret Thatcher, a mere back-bencher.

Most of the affluent audience, elegant ladies most of them, beamed at the blonde Conservative politician on the platform while scowling at the rest of us. Or they did so at first.

But Margaret the Mouth – as she would be called in Wales – sounded off at a hell of a rate. When a question about architecture was read out by the chairman, the famous architect on the panel seemed set to reply. He had not bargained for Margaret the Mouth.

Ten minutes later a question was posed about the poetry of W. H. Auden. It was evidently designed for me. I was too slow. The dominant voice began: 'When I was at Oxford, W. H. Auden. . .' The audience by this time had turned off their beam.

Arriving home I told my wife Joan: 'Today I met a politician with so little sense of audience she'll never get anywhere though she seems ambitious.' Again I was sure I was right.

Because of my own inability to prophesy correctly I have not much time for magicians. The only one I truly admire has been dead these many years. He was Tyridales, the King of Armenia, who, asked to prophesy for Nero, travelled all the way by land because he believed it sinful to spit into the sea or otherwise discharge into it 'that which might pollute and defile that Element'.

A magician such as he should be made director of British Nuclear Fuels.

'Convictions are prisons.' So they may be and it's odd that the word 'convict' should resemble the word 'conviction'. I have been reading how Trotsky, in 1929, looking back, confessed that 'the feeling of the supremacy of the general over the particular, of law over fact, of theory over personal experience, took root in my mind at an early age and gained increasing strength as the years advanced'.

How repugnant that is. Don't most of us feel the contrary? Don't we feel the supremacy of the particular over the general, of fact over law, of personal experience over theory

I took the record off – a Beethoven piano sonata – and I sat in the armchair thinking of nothing in particular. I did not even notice the silence after music. I sat there contentedly until the door opened. 'What's the matter?' she asked. I did not reply. 'You're depressed,' she said. I did not contradict her though I wanted to smile at her presumption.

I should have told her that my face misleadingly assumes, in repose, a melancholy aspect. Instead I stared at her without expression.

At once she spoke with such sympathy, such sweetness, such softness, that gradually I began to feel sorrowful. 'What have you got to be so sad about?' she asked. 'You're lucky. You've got so many things going for you. You should thank God. . .' I interrupted her. I felt that I should have a reason or two for my face, in repose, registering that fake despondency.

'It's 1984,' I remarked, implying that Old Age, like the Post Office, was just around the corner. 'And the leaders of all the nations are so reactionary, near the night borders of insanity as a matter of fact, that it's frightening. Why, if one of those psychopaths punched the button. . . .'

She ceased frowning. She wanted to cheer me up, I could see that. She picked up the record I had not put away – the Beethoven sonata. 'This is so beautiful,' she said. 'Listen to this. It will raise your spirits.'

I sat there hearing Brendel playing again and soon I was restored, felt contented as before. Then I noticed, half way through the largo e mesto, how sad and serious her face had become.

Each morning, somewhere in York, a certain Mr and Mrs Brown eagerly turn to an inside page of *The Times*. They are intent upon listing the names of children whose birth or adoption has been announced in those august columns. Each January they complete a League Table of the most popular names given, obviously by the Right People, to boys and girls the previous year.

This January, 1984, they tell us *James* has won again. He's been top of the Boys' League now for twenty years. *Elizabeth* has also, during 1983, scored the most in the Girls' League. She's only been champion for a mere eight years. Royal rather than Hollywood names dominate these Leagues. There are no Carys or Craigs or Mias.

In a recently published book of his *Selected Prose* (Poetry Wales Press) the Welsh Nationalist poet, R. S. Thomas, proudly announces that his son's name is *Gwydion*. No common or garden James or Charles for R. S. Thomas. As a result, though, of his choosing a name so fancy and so Welsh, people continually ask, 'What does the name mean?' Not unfairly, the Rev. R. S. Thomas complains, 'They'd never ask me what William or Margaret meant.'

He goes on to say, 'Our ancestors tended religiously to avoid giving pagan names to their children for fear they might exert an evil influence upon them. As a result, our nation is overloaded with names like John and Mary. It puts a strain on one's belief in the immortality of the individual to cast an eye over the old church registers and see the number of John Jones' and Mary Roberts' who have passed over the faces of Wales like the shadow of a cloud.'

Welsh or not, we all have a 'thing' about names. Primitive man knew that his name was an integral part of his personality, a fraction of his soul. So do we, in a less defined way. Rationally I may know that a rose is a rose and would smell as sweet had it any other name. Deep down, though, I don't believe it.

On the contrary, I know, within the depths of myself, that if all roses were called, say, gwydions, these flowers would then tell a different story, their perfume would be quite other, they would smell like nothing else that has ever been.

Do our names not contribute to our destinies? Is it an accident, for instance, that the Director of Waterworks and Sewage in Glamorgan – I'm not making this up – should own the surname of Lillycrap? And that the noted author of *The Psychoanalysis of Culture* and other such Freudian analytical works should be no other than a Dr Badcock?

My Uncle Max, now aged eighty-nine, grumbled because of his arthritis. He then quite seriously proclaimed, 'You know, Dan, it's a pity we can't suffer our illnesses when we're young and healthy.'

At a party, the other evening, I heard another 'Sam Goldwynism'. A *Sunday Express* journalist was talking about the loyalty of his editor, Sir John Junor, to his staff. One journalist, though, apparently received the boot. Sir John complained, 'Sometimes your copy is brilliant, other times it's awful. What I want is consistent mediocrity.'

One actual Sam Goldwyn anecdote I have long relished concerns Billy Wilder who wanted to make a film about Nijinsky. He went to Sam Goldwyn and related how the dancer ended up in a Swiss mental home believing himself to be a horse. Sam Goldwyn was far from impressed. He said, 'You're crazy. That's too downbeat. Who would want to see a movie about a man who thought he was a horse?'

Billy Wilder shrugged his shoulders. 'It could have a happy ending,' he declared. 'We could show that horse winning the Derby.'

I have been unable to finish *Schindler's Ark*, the Booker prize 'novel' of 1982 which is now in paperback. I found it too painful. Oddly, last month, I was able to sit through the television programme about Schindler despite those too true, horrific shots where corpses who seemed to have risen from the Post-Mortem slab walked towards the camera with huge eyes.

Schindler was a strange kind of seedy hero. When the programme concluded I turned to my bookcase to reread an essay by Schopenhauer where he talks about the motives of so-called good actions. According to that pessimistic philosopher, disinterested, noble kindness exists but rarely. If the individual carrying out the good brave deed does not do so blindly because of the moral codes imposed upon him by Society then his actions are generally performed in the unformulated or concrete hope of some reward – if not in this world, then in the next.

Yet Schopenhauer is not entirely cynical. For instance, he finds precious a common engraving illustrating a true scene. It is of a soldier kneeling in front of a firing squad. The soldier is waving a cloth to frighten away his dog that wishes to come to him. Sentimental? Engravings of many selfless common acts in our hospitals would seem as much.

In Brussels, the interpreters locked in their glass-windowed cages were busy, mouth and hand, while poets from the EEC each day, in turn, pontificated on the present trends of poetry in Germany, France, Italy, Greece, Belgium, Luxembourg, Britain and Ireland. (For some reason the Dutch poet didn't turn up. Drunk possibly?) After each lecture a discussion followed. The lectures were unremarkable, the interpreters fantastic, the large audience as patient as fishermen.

The second morning, my stint over, I sat with headphones on, listening to the Flemish poet, Eddy Van Vliet. Afterwards, a hand was raised by an elderly man who looked benign – rather like a plump, rosy-cheeked Father Christmas without a beard. His speech, however, was blunt. 'Your survey of modern Flemish poetry was no good,' he said. 'Hopeless. For instance, you left me out.'

Poets, I decided, were the same the world over. All, whatever their nationality, felt neglected. So that was why I was smiling at the Flemish Father Christmas poet. 'It's not as simple as that,'

Eddy Van Vliet whispered to me later. 'You see, that fellow was once head of the SS in Belgium. He was imprisoned for war crimes. There were political undertones to his objections.' I found myself staring at the interpreters busy behind the glass. I did not have my headphones on. I could not hear what they were saying.

One cannot eat in peace in a Brussels restaurant. You sit at a table reading the mouth-watering menu – at least it would be mouth-watering if you could understand it. Before the waiter returns to take your order a loud-clothed gentleman appears. He looks like George Melly. He is not George Melly. He has a basket of orchids and he is offering one to your companion. 'For the beautiful lady,' he says in three languages. He waits smiling. You do not wish to be stingy. Your right hand is furtive, searching for money. The lady is smiling, the George Melly man is smiling, you show your teeth.

The waiter arrives. You order Potage du Jour not only because it is the cheapest item on the menu but also because you can actually pronounce it reasonably. Your companion is suddenly seized with a Hamlet-sized doubt. The Moules Marinière or the Coquilles Saint-Jacques à la Parisienne? She dithers for a whole act. First it's this, then it's that, then it's this, last it's that.

The waiter quits with a dazed look. Never mind, several big laughs later we actually begin our meal when, good heavens, who should enter but The Charming Young Artist flogging his prints. Horribly, the lady seems to take an interest in (a) Movement without Force and (b) Untitled. 'Which do you prefer?' she asks. Your teeth ache, exposed to so much unaccustomed oxygen.

Before coffee you are solicited by a Salvation Army lady, a Lottery ticket seller and, inexplicably, by a comedian trying to sell you – I swear to God – a packet of nuts. He will not go away. He is making the joke with the beautiful lady. You are already wishing you were back home visiting The Great Nepalese Restaurant (recommended, of course, by Fay Maschler) having a quiet tête à tête with your beloved, enjoying the onion bhaji, the chicken tikka, the mutton dopiaza, the shahi kharma. 'We'll be home tomorrow,' you say to the beautiful lady. And you are smiling.

*

At the football match one unsmiling spectator near me kept on obsessively swearing for the full ninety minutes plus extra time. He swore at his own team, at the visiting players, at the linesmen and, most of all, at the referee. *Discriminate* swearing is one thing, but this was too much. I wanted to shout out, 'Shut your bloody mouth.'

I do not believe that my objection to *obsessive* swearing is because of a prissy upbringing. True, when I was a boy in South Wales, our house remained reasonably oath-free. My mother never shouted in anger anything less refined than 'damn it' or 'Helen of Troy' or 'that dirty dog'; and my father also refused to allow himself, at home anyway, the vivid, improper consolations of a barrack-room vocabulary. Still, my elder brothers let fly now and then.

Who was the first man to swear, I wonder? Adam, probably. I imagine him amiably naming the animals, becoming rather bored by it and adding a robust, forbidden adjective here, an expletive there, to describe, if not the sheep and the goats, at least the stinking vulture and the noxious snake. After all, what word could the fellow utter when his head was excreted on by the fowls of heaven?

I cannot remember which reliable source reported that one sunlit, bell-ringing, car-washing, Sunday morning, the gods came down from the mountains, walked into our towns under the leafy pavement trees, and entered the cool darkness of our churches. There they stood up when the congregation stood up, kneeled when the congregation kneeled. The service over, they quit these churches as men.

It seems that nowadays some ex-gods are called ex-Prime Ministers. They are shunned somewhat by present Members of Parliament. It is as if their clothes still reek of the pungent smoke of ancient sacrificial fires. We, mere mortals, cannot endure the smell.

For instance, when Harold Wilson resigned his godhood, after attending one of these church services, I am told that fellow MPs in the lobbies, treated him like an untreated leper. He became a lonely, even a pathetic figure. Obviously it takes a long time for sacerdotal, stale odours to wear away and for a god to become wholly human. Being a compassionate chap, I cannot help but be sorry for their families.

Is Mary Wilson, for instance, happier for being married to one descended from on high? I bet the capricious public no longer buy her books of verse in such quantities as once they did. Still I find it hard to cry about that. I recall clearly Sir Robert Lusty, then the Managing Director of Hutchinson, moaning, 'Your *Collected Poems* are not selling as well as Mary Wilson's.' I had to reply, 'I would have to marry Ted Heath to do as well as she does.' In those days Ted Heath still had angels' wings beating the air about him. He was not yet a fully qualified mortal. That was why, surely, my remark made Sir Robert Lusty look so bereft of leaves. Things are different now, to be sure, Mr Heath is, at last, on the way to achieving a reverse apotheosis. Look how he is treated by the newspapers.

The other day, as he ate his egg, he must have read the headline in *The Times*: HEATH'S COLLEAGUES ACCUSE HIM OF DISLOYALTY IN VOTE. Apparently, these colleagues are all called Anon. 'Mr Heath's decision,' wrote *The Times*' political reporter, Philip Webster, 'to vote against the Government over its rate-capping legislation has upset some of his closest parliamentary colleagues. . . .'

Who? '. . . most notably Cabinet ministers who served under him when he was Prime Minister. . . .'

Who? 'Ministers who remain sympathetic to Mr Heath's economic views are privately critical of him. . . .'

Who? 'One Cabinet Minister who has always been closer to Mr Heath than to Margaret Thatcher.'

Who? Mr Webster names no names. It seems that anonymous, mephitic figures, men who have never been christened have whispered into his hairy ear.

The trouble is that Ted Heath forgets he is an ex-god. Now and then he proclaims holy things about the way the present government continues to dismantle our Welfare State. He remarks from the mountain, 'We can afford to care. We have never been able to afford not to.' Disgraceful fellow, what?

I received in the post a communication from a Mr John Sumsion, the Registrar of Public Lending Rights. I now know how much

I have earned between July '82 and July '83 as a result of my books being borrowed from the free libraries of Great Britain.

I can't help but wonder if I have done better than Mary Wilson.

Apparently, of the 16 sample libraries monitored one was the Hendon Central Library. I console myself I would have done better had one or another Hampstead Library been selected. After all, I have no friends or relatives living in Hendon. The Uncle who once did so – my Uncle Isaac Shepherd – has for some years borrowed his books from the stacks of Eternity.

Had Uncle still been alive he undoubtedly would have made regular visits to Hendon Central Library to take out my books for my sake. As a matter of fact he was the only person I know who seemed delighted when, twenty or so years ago, we moved from our cramped flat in Belsize Park to our house in Golders Green. Then, with the innocence of extreme narcissism, he remarked, 'That's better, Dannie. Now you're more central.'

But the death of my Uncle Isaac is not the only reason why I did not scoop the PLR jackpot. I feel sure it is because of my surname. There is no gainsaying that if you happen to be an author it is a disadvantage to own a name beginning with A. If you are among the L's – Larkin, Lessing, Laurie Lee, Levi-Strauss – you can't miss, you are at supermarket eye level. But the As are way up high, out of sight, out of reach. You have to be a giant to read Abse. On the other hand you have to be a dwarf to read Wilson.

When my Uncle Isaac expressed his approval of my move from NW3 to NW11, I did not know the Talmudic story of that disputatious rabbi, Joshua ben Hanania and the Greek philosophers – otherwise I would have told it to him. I imagine Rabbi Joshua as a small man with a long beard that almost touched his feet. The Athenians, no doubt, with whom he was arguing, were taller and bald. 'Where,' demanded one of that bald number, 'where, Rabbi, is the centre of the earth? In Jerusalem? In Corinth? Syracuse? Damascus? Carthage? Memphis? Antioch? Tyre? Thebes?'

Rabbi Joshua, unadvised by Uncle Isaac, did not know he should have replied, 'Hendon.' (Why else, by the way, is the Tube station called Hendon Central?) Instead, smiley-sweet,

Rabbi Joshua pointed at the greenish stony ground beneath him. 'If you doubt me,' he said to those scowling bald philosophers, 'bring your apparatus, bring long rods, bring rope, bring all the string of Athens and measure it for yourselves.'

I am not alone in believing my local park, Golders Hill Park, with its peacocks, llamas and emus etc., to be one of the most pleasant in London. Yet the park remains relatively unknown. One who enjoyed it earlier this century was W. H. Hudson (1841–1922). He often strolled this way with such a literary Hampstead friend as Ernest Rhys, the editor of the Everyman Library.

Yesterday afternoon the park spread out cold and moody and empty. I walked up its green slopes past the stark black trees towards the abandoned bandstand and the little pond near the walled flower garden. Arriving at that pond I read the red board with its white painted admonition: DANGER, THIN ICE. And standing, asleep, one-legged on the ice, their heads beneath wings, stood the four flamingoes that I had come to visit.

Each winter I observe this odd, dream-like scene enacted. On each occasion, W. H. Hudson's description of a flamingo killing in Patagonia comes to mind. He wrote how he, carrying a gun and accompanied by his dog, encountered a small flock of flamingoes in a lagoon. He wrote, 'I crept up to the rushes in a fever of excitement; not that flamingoes are not common in this district, but because I had noticed that one of the birds before me was the largest and loveliest flamingo I had ever set eyes on. . . I think my hand trembled a great deal; nevertheless the bird dropped when I fired.'

How dare Hudson have killed such a benign creature? If he had not admired it that flamingo would have lived out its blameless natural life. Nowadays, each winter, I turn angrily from the frozen pond to look for the phantom of W. H. Hudson. Yesterday afternoon I surely heard, in the distance, his ghost screech thin with grief. Else it was the startled cry of a peacock.

February 1984

This morning, at the chest clinic, where I now work only part-time – sessional work, Mondays, Tuesdays – my first patient was under surveillance because some years ago he had been exposed to crocidolite dust (blue asbestos). He had no chest symptoms and the X-rays continued to show the lung fields to be clear. I stood before the blazing X-ray screens and turned to tell him the happy news.

He was not surprised. He had no problems with his chest. His concern was with his legs and feet. 'They're getting worse, doctor,' he explained. He told me in detail the nature of his symptoms, when they came on, their intensity and duration, and I told him that his symptoms had nothing to do with his exposure to asbestos.

After I had examined him I half-wondered whether he suffered from what was once called Buerger's Disease. In 1908, a certain Dr Buerger described this rather rare condition and suggested that it was a disease confined to Polish Jews. Forty years later that was what I was taught, it being current medical dogma so many text-books ago, when I was a medical student at Westminster Hospital.

Then, remarkably, King George VI was diagnosed as suffering from the disease.

At once, those medical text-books had to be rewritten, Stalinised as it were. No longer was Buerger's Disease one that attacked Polish Jews particularly. Statements suggesting it did so were erased from the page. The very term, 'Buerger's Disease', became unfashionable. Rather, its scientific name, Thrombo-Angiitis Obliterans came into favour. The fame of poor old Dr Buerger, in Britain anyway, began to fade. Posthumously he was in the dog-house.

What about my patient? There is such a thing as medical confidentiality. I'll tell you this though: my patient was circumcised.

Whenever I observe Margaret Thatcher on TV I have the uneasy feeling she is wearing a mask. Images of politicians are not simply invented by media hacks and by PR hirelings as some seem to believe. The making of a politician's image, his or her mask, is a strange communal enterprise in which we, the public, participate and in which the principal actively takes part.

And it is not only the images of politicians that are delivered into being this way. So it is for all public figures, be they kings and queens, bastards or bards. No wonder our sense of historical reality is so fragile and that the more we investigate the past the more we discover it to be mythological. But then, all of us wear some disguise – except those who are crying.

Margaret Thatcher, for some years now, has been cast as the Iron Lady. She accepts that image and helps to perpetuate it. 'I have an iron determination,' she recently declared in Hungary. If nothing else, she is determined to be determined and many are those who admire her, like her that way. I suspect that Mrs Thatcher's habitual impersonation of herself has become her true nature. The mask has become her face.

But has she not also allowed herself another role in which she extols Victorian values? There is no contradiction. It was a Victorian, Oscar Wilde, who averred that the first duty in life is to be as artificial as possible. Oscar Wilde continued, 'What the second is no one has yet discovered.'

A confession. On weekday afternoons, if I do not engage myself in dutiful or honourable activities such as working, or at least serious reading, then I experience a sense of unease. The ghost in the mirror points his finger at me. I used to suffer those same feelings on the occasions when, as a wayward medical student, I deliberately missed a lecture or a ward round, to spend instead a guilty afternoon at the Swiss Cottage Odeon.

By Wednesday lunchtime, though, I yearned for a wicked game of chess. So I telephoned my friend, the pipe-smoking LSE philosopher, John Watkins, who lives in Erskine Hill, Hampstead Garden Suburb.

'OK,' Professor Watkins agreed philosophically, 'if you come over here.'

The sky was high and February blue, the sun low, the light peculiarly bright and liquid as if reflected from cutlery. I walked down Finchley Road to turn up Hoop Lane, conscious that it was a lovely day. I felt curiously cheerful. Then, as I approached the railings of the cemetery, I observed in front of me the first black hearse with its flower-covered coffin, parked opposite the Crematorium gate.

Behind the hearse, another stationary, black limousine waited by the kerb. Three people sat bolt upright in the back, unsmiling, motionless, not talking to each other. They owned the melancholy faces of sleepers, except their eyes were open, their mouths shut. I walked on towards the roundabout.

Then came, silent as a conspiracy, a second funeral cortège. First the long car with the fresh coffin, followed by another shining, black automobile, chauffeur-driven. And in the back seat, again, three mourners sat upright, neither looking to the right nor to the left. They had similar despondent faces. I looked over my shoulder and saw behind me the parked, mourning car with its first three occupants and suddenly a possible line for a poem came into my head: 'Some talk in their sleep very few sing.'

Some talk in their sleep, very few sing. I thought about that and a few more matching lines occurred to me so that as I walked on I struggled to get the sound of the meaning right. The funerals had set me ticking – as Sylvia Plath said in a different context – 'set me ticking like a fat gold watch'. Why not? The theme of Death is to Poetry what Mistaken Identity is to Drama.

But then those nascent lines in my head became derailed, as if I had been button-holed by a man from Porlock. For on the other side of the roundabout a third hearse with coffin approached. From poetic trance I was jolted into the ordinary, beautiful, common air of a particular Wednesday afternoon and was astonished.

For it was as if, from diverse corners of London, funeral cars were converging to this focal point in Golders Green and each hearse, in its turn, with its chauffeur of Death, had to wait, had to idle the minutes away, rather like an aeroplane circling and circling, not given clearance to land at some crowded airport.

However, behind the third, so-controlled cortege came, at last, another car – one not sleek, one as a matter of fact battered, shabby, and driven neither by a ceremonial chauffeur, nor carrying three exhausted occupants in the back. The driver was young and the window next to him wound down so that, out of it, came the raucous noise of Radio One. The young driver had evidently turned the knob of his radio on to half past six because the volume of this so-called music was startlingly loud, spectacularly loud.

I was not offended. I welcomed this pollution of silence. For that blaring noise celebrated, there and then, informality, youth, vivid life. For some reason I could not understand, as I progressed into Hampstead Garden suburb, I felt confident that that afternoon I was going to win my game of chess.

Great activity in the house. My son, David, is framing his prints and drawings for his first exhibition which he is to share later this month with the gifted young painter, Sue Morris, at the Leigh Gallery in Bloomsbury.

Over our bread and cheese lunch we talked, my wife, myself, and David, about the expertise of Art Critics. My wife declared she had a high regard for some critics, among them Edward Lucie Smith and John Russell Taylor. My son seemed more sceptical. He related to us the story of one, Soderini, who, while praising the colossal statue of David, complained to Michelangelo that the nose was too thick.

'So Michelangelo,' my son continued, 'took a chisel in one hand and a scoop of marble dust in the other. Then he climbed the scaffolding around the statue. Reaching the top he pretended to chip away at the criticised nose and, while doing so, allowed marble dust to filter from his hand. On climbing down again, he asked Soderini what he thought now. 'So much better,' the critic said: 'so much better, you've given it life.'

My son stood up and asked me if I wished to look at 'the stuff' he was putting into the exhibition. I nodded. I was going to be very very careful about making any critical remarks whatsoever about *my* David.

Why do young people slam the front door with such passionate intensity? You can tell the age of an individual not by inspecting their teeth but rather by how loudly they slam the front door shut. The youngest in our family had just stepped out of the front porch, leaving our house shaking as if it were in Beirut. No matter, I dusted the ceiling flakes from my shoulders and, in the returning silence, worked away happily.

Then our cat, Caitlin, suddenly exploded. She alighted on my desk – a prodigious leap – scattering my papers. She made it plain that she wished to be fed. Since my wife would not be home for hours yet, since everyone else, one by one, had quit the house with loud ostentation, there was only me around to provide, damn it.

When I reached the kitchen, intent on opening a tin of cat meat, the hall turned nasty. Or rather its sole occupant did – the telephone. 'All right, all *right*,' I yelled, 'I'm coming.'

Eleven paces later, I picked up the receiver and a voice in it peremptorily demanded, 'Is that Dannie Abse?'

'Yes,' I admitted.

'The great poet, Dannie Abse.'

Oh heck, I thought. This was no relative.

'Hunter Davies,' the voice continued, 'this is Hunter Davies. I think your column in the Ham and High is fan*tastic*.'

I hesitated. I had met Hunter Davies once. He had seemed pleasant enough, he hadn't gone over the top then. Was this *the* Hunter Davies?

'We're not being recorded,' he said confidentially. What did he mean we weren't being recorded?

'What do you mean "we're not being recorded?" ' I asked this Bulgarian spy, Hunter Davies.

He explained. He was doing a programme called Bookshelf for Radio 4 and he was telephoning different authors to record their reactions to the Public Lending Right results, those who had become enriched by thousands of pounds and those, apparently, such as myself who could now buy an extra tin of cat meat.

'I just want you to repeat the things you said in your Ham and High column, OK?' he ordered.

I tried to recall what I had written for the Ham and High some weeks back. The cat, meanwhile, had come into the hall and was looking at me reproachfully with both her eyes.

'OK, is it?' said Hunter Davies louder.

'OK,' I said to the cat who was still salivating away and looking as despondent as coitus interruptus.

Then the phone went dead. I waited. Nothing happened. Hunter Davies, I thought, why when he had just now given me

18

all those verbal medals, I should have responded in kind. 'Not *the* Hunter Davies,' I should have babbled. 'Not the author of that simply magic book that I so admired and liked and cherished, *The Glory Game?*'

Ignoring the cat who was now rubbing herself against my left leg, I crooned down the telephone-receiver that have gone dead, 'My God, that Wordsworth book you wrote, Hunter Davies, was OUT OF THIS WORLD. And your book, *The Joy of Stamps*, was a masterpiece.'

'Sorry to keep you, Dr Abse,' a woman's voice said on the suddenly alive phone. 'This is the producer. We'll be ready to record shortly.' I nodded. I don't think she heard me nod.

Then, to my dismay, the front door bell rang. Since the phone was silent again I dashed to the door and opened it. 'I've come to service the gas-boiler,' said the man standing and staring there. 'Come in,' I said. 'I won't be a moment, I'm on the phone.'

He stood in the hall. The cat stood in the hall. I stood in the hall, holding the telephone receiver. I was about to ask the man from the North Thames Gas Board if he would mind feeding the cat when the woman producer said, making me jump, 'We're ready now, Dr Abse.'

Some profoundly shocking experiments are being performed at The Chemical Warfare Centre at Porton Down in Wiltshire. The victims of these experiments are monkeys, rabbits, sheep, pigs, rats, mice, as well as, possibly, dogs and cats.

The Junior Defence Minister, John Lee, recently admitted that each year, (repeat, each year) in Britain, 10,000 animal experiments are conducted by the Ministry of Defence. Sheep, for instance, have been shot in wounding tests – the Government being interested, so we are told, in the wounding efficacy of ammunition.

No doubt many would think me absurd when I confess that such facts remind me of the medical atrocity experiments of the Nazis in 1942 at the Ravensbruck Concentration Camp for women.

The subjects there, they would needlessly remind me, were human.

Karl Gebhardt, head physician of the Hohenlychen Orthopaedic Clinic and President of the German Red Cross would not have assented to that judgement. He believed his victims to be sub-human, to be animals.

Dr Gebhardt, along with his assistant, Dr Fritz Fischer, inflicted deep surgical wounds on healthy young women before introducing into the wounds a mixed infection containing septic gas-gangrene organisms and earth.

Pure sadism. Is shooting sheep not sadism?

The scientists at Porton Down would not accept that their experiments are sadistic. They would argue that their results will help in the treatment of wounded soldiers should there be a war.

Nor would Gebhardt and Fischer have accepted the verdict of sadism. By subsequently giving their female 'animals' the then new sulphonamide drugs they felt they would discover the value of such therapy before prescribing it for noble German soldiers wounded on the Eastern Front.

The fact is all victims are described as worthless, as a form of vermin, by their persecutors – if the victims be human then they are perceived as being sub-human; if animals, then they are considered as creatures with little or no intelligence.

When I was a second year medical student studying physiology I liked and admired our professor – Professor MacDowell. I enjoyed his sardonic humour. He once remarked that Life consisted of three instincts, the three Fs: Fear, Food and Reproduction. His office was on the fifth floor where he would occasionally carry out tests on heart patients. Frequently, in those days, the lift broke down and those patients had to climb the steep stairs to his office. He never examined them when they arrived. 'If they're not dead when they reach me,' he used to say, 'their hearts are OK.'

Yes, I was amused by Professor MacDowell. But one day, for the benefit of the second year medical students, he carried out experiments on an anaesthetised, dissected cat. When some of us objected our professor assured us that cats had no intelligence worth talking about. 'They are worthless creatures,' he taught the nineteen year old medical students. For years I believed him, I believed that cats were truly stupid. (Sorry, Caitlin.)

No doubt scientists at Porton Down have found it necessary to have a similar contempt for sheep. What I feel sure of is that Gebhardt and Fischer would have felt very comfortable working at that secret green and pleasant spot in bird-trilling Wiltshire, England, 1984.

They were streaming out of Dunstan Road synagogue in Golders Green as I happened to be passing by. I overheard one bearded man say to another, 'One thing I wanted to say about the soul. . . .' I slowed my pace in order to follow their theological speculations '. . . is that it does tend to come away from the uppers.'

March 1984

On my way home I read the newspaper placard: TITO GOBBI DIES IN ROME. Immediately I thought of my Uncle Joe – my favourite among the many brothers of my mother. Joe had told me how, one evening while on holiday in Italy, he had wandered into the hotel bar. In no time at all he found himself in conversation with an Italian gentleman.

'No, no, I was born in Bassano del Grappo in the Veneto region,' said the stranger. 'But I like this part of Italy.'

'I was born in Ystalyfera in South Wales, ' offered my gregarious uncle.

Soon they were exchanging views about politics, about the relative qualities of Rome and London, about Napoleon Bonaparte, icthyology, the internal combustion engine, Shakespeare, celestial photography and one or two other ordinary conversational topics.

After another drink my uncle, curious about his new-found friend, remarked, 'I'm a doctor, you know. I have a practice in Hampstead Garden suburb in London. What, sir, do you do for a living?'

The Italian replied, smiling, 'I'm Tito Gobbi.' My uncle extended his hand. 'My name is Joe Shepherd. But, as I said, what do you do for a living?'

'I'm Tito Gobbi,' Tito Gobbi repeated, his smile retreating.

My uncle decided that the stranger's English was, after all, somewhat deficient. 'Signor Gobbi,' my uncle now deliberated very slowly and clearly, enunciating each word so that he could be understood, 'What ... do ... you ... do ... for ... a ... living?'

Joe Shepherd went on to tell me how the fellow unaccountably bolted for the exit.

My uncle, a first-class general physician, a most capable diagnostician, could identify patients' diseases with precision. But he wasn't so hot at identifying the names of the patients themselves.

There was that time when we were in a theatre foyer and James Mason hovered nearby. Because Mr Mason looked familiar to my uncle he assumed the film star was a patient of his.

'Feeling better?' he asked James Mason.

The actor stopped in his tracks. 'Thank you,' he said. My uncle nodded. 'You look better since you've had the treatment,' he added. James Mason looked over his shoulder rather wildly, I thought, as he ascended the staircase.

One summer afternoon, when I was nineteen, I entered a tobacconist's in Swiss Cottage and asked as usual for a packet of twenty Players. The proprietor of this small shop obviously had no commercial sense for he replied, 'You shouldn't smoke. It stops you from growing. You could grow as tall as Romeo.'

That was how I knew Romeo was a tall guy. I was only 5' 8½", not much bigger than my Uncle Joe. Years later, when I was also a doctor, I wished I had taken the tobacconist's advice. Not because I wanted to be like Romeo but because I observed too many pulmonary cripples who had become such as a result of the chronic irritation of tobacco smoke. There I sat at my desk in the chest clinic, hurriedly putting out my cigarette, as I recommended patients to give up smoking completely.

I had tried to stop smoking a number of times. My own father had been killed by tobacco's lethal effects. I had looked at his chest X-ray that day in 1964 and seen above the left hemidiaphragm a shadow that should not have been there, that was, I knew, a malignant growth, a cancer.

For years after that, whenever I looked at an X-ray on a bright, lit screen, my eyes would be drawn to a particular location above the left hemi-diaphragm.

Then during Christmas time, 1968, a wonderful thing happened. I suffered a severe influenza. For days I did not want to smoke and when I began to recover I managed to kick the habit. I'm glad I did so. Multitudes have been killed by cigarettes since then. It has been estimated that over the last quarter of a century a million people in Britain alone have died because of tobacco-induced diseases – cancer, heart disease, contraceptive pill complications etc.

Now, at last, the British people are catching on. February 29th was Stop Smoking Day. And now Nigel Lawson has done his Budget bit – though he could have done more. In any case, the British are giving up smoking in their thousands, in their tens of thousands, in their hundreds of thousands. The statistics reveal this.

Even inconsequential surveys such as those carried out by the Dateline Computer Agency show that most women on their books desire not only a medium-built young male between 5'9" and 6' but one who is also a non-smoker. That tobacconist was right, Romeo was tall and had no smoker's cough.

However, though as a nation we are giving up the habit of smoking, the tobacco companies based here and in the USA are clawing back their profits. They are exporting their little packets of delayed death to the Third World.

The *Lancet* has reported how some brands, along with those manufactured under licence overseas, 'have a much higher tar and nicotine content than those smoked at home'.

Six years ago a World Health Organisation document advised that, 'In the absence of strong and resolute government action, we face the serious probability that the smoking epidemic will have affected the developing world within a decade.' Already there is a rising and alarming casualty list in India, Pakistan, the Philippines, China, Hong Kong and Cuba. It is sad to see snap-shots of children in these countries smoking and smiling so innocently.

I should not have mocked Joe Shepherd's occasional inability to recognise people. I have just come back to London after finishing a BBC-TV *Return Journey* film in Cardiff. At one point I was required to walk into a house in Whitchurch Road where I was born.

As I waited outside for John Geraint, the director, to give me the signal to start walking to the front door, a bespectacled stranger came towards me smiling warmly. His face seemed familiar. Some old schoolmate, perhaps?

Ignoring the TV crew, he said, 'Hello, hello, how are you? You do recognise me, Dan?'

A sudden illumination. 'Of course, Stanley,' I said triumphantly. 'You haven't changed.'

He hesitated. 'Colin,' he said.

How strange to enter the bedroom where one was born. I tried to imagine my mother lying in the bed, the midwife announcing, 'It's a boy,' and the baby who was me crying like billyo.

I have been told that when I was born my eldest brother, Wilfred, aged eight, went out and bought me a *Comic Cuts* to read. My other brother, Leo, six years old, not to be outdone, superiorly announced, 'I'll buy him *The Children's Newspaper*.' I can reveal now there is no truth in the report that I pushed the *Comic Cuts* away, shouting 'Rubbish' or that I immediately rejected *The Children's Newspaper* as being inaccurate.

Afterwards, I went downstairs into the kitchen. I shut my eyes and tried to remember something, anything – the noise of peas being shelled, peas falling into a resonant zinc bucket; or of gas hissing until the sound of a paper bag exploded over a stove. But I heard nothing. I opened my eyes and saw only what was there. . . .

Later that day the TV crew followed me past my old elementary school and I recalled how it used to be. There was a war going on in Spain; one of Leo's friends, Sid Hamm, had been killed out there, fighting for the International Brigade; Mussolini was puffed out and ranting in Italy; Hitler, dangerously maniacal in Germany. There was sloth and unemployment in the Welsh valleys and the Prince of Wales had said poshly, uselessly, 'Something must be done.' But nothing was done.

At school we sang, 'Let the prayer re-echo, God Bless the Prince of Wales,' though I mistakenly believed that patriotic lyric to be, 'Let the prairie echo, God Bless the Prince of Wales,' and wondered vaguely where the devil were those grass-waving prairies in mountainous Wales.

Of course, it's all different now, in 1984: there is no unemployment in South Wales, there are no dictators or wars anywhere in the world, the Prince of Wales has a different face, God's in his heaven, all's right with the world.

The lady from Hampstead CND told me that on April 7th at 2 p.m. there would be a march past buildings named in the 'Camden War Plan'. The march would culminate in a 'die-in' at the Whitestone Pond. So, at the Pond, would I read that poem I had once written about the possibility of a nuclear holocaust?

Indeed, I had written such a poem. I had written it in the 1950s at the height of the then Cold War. But what did she mean by a 'die-in'? She informed me how everybody would lie down signifying that the Heath was planned as Hampstead's Mass Grave.

It would be easy to mock such symbolic measures. One could, though, just as well pour scorn on the wreath-laying ceremony at the Whitehall Cenotaph on November 11th. After all, one ritual is a public lament for war casualties of the past while the other is for possible casualties of a catastrophic future.

On the other hand, like so many of the silent majority, I dislike participating in public protests, especially if one is asked to be ostentatious in them. I wish I did not feel that way, but I do. I wish that I was not so hesitant about signing petitions, joining protest marches, however just. No doubt, part of my reluctance is the result of my bourgeois upbringing with its concern for What Will the Neighbours Think? I hope it's more than that. I do have the sense that a poet's importance, such as it minimally is, lies in his or her poetry, and gesturing on public platforms is too often a mere theatrical, hollow enterprise.

'So will you read your poem?' requested the lady from CND.

'Yes,' I said, wishing she had not asked me in the first place.

A thousand years ago the bard sat at the right hand of his Welsh prince and spoke for the prince; now, princes such as they are, disguised with other names, have no use for bards, at least not in our part of the world. And elsewhere, in certain countries in South America, or in Eastern Europe for instance, the bard is more likely, being subversive by nature, to be thrown into a dungeon or a mental hospital by those who have the power of princes, than to sit honoured at their polished tables.

Camus wrote, 'The writer's role is not free of difficult duties. By definition he cannot put himself today in the service of those who make history; he is at the service of those who suffer it.' Even Camus' remark is an exaggerated statement. The writer, after all, is not separate from those who suffer the active decisions of the princes. He suffers them himself and so whatever he does publicly is self-serving.

What a bother, you may think, simply because you've been asked to read a poem at the Whitestone Pond. Quite right. If someone had asked me to read out the same poem in Moscow I would have said, 'No.' I would have been too scared.

One of my two daughters, Susanna, has been travelling around the world with a friend since last August. Letters arrive from strange places – Thailand, India, Japan. She seems to be enjoying her adventure and will surely be enriched by it, but selfishly I'm beginning to miss her. There simply aren't enough people around this house for me to tell off or to ask, 'Who's the Best Driver in the World?'

So I wish Susanna, now that April is coming, would have some Home Thoughts from Abroad. How can I induce enough nostalgia in her to make a return journey imperative and soon? I shall send her a postcard naming names. I shall speak of the daffodils in Golders Hill Park; the fair at Hampstead Heath; the unexpected bit of canal at Camden Lock; the elegance of Ken Wood; the delightful curve downhill of Fitzjohn's Avenue; the cherry blossom that will soon arrive on the trees of Golders Green like so many bits of the *Financial Times*.

How can she resist the power of nostalgia? Peter Vansittart told me a story I can never forget. It concerned a Chinese general who once – defending a city beseiged by the Mongols and with no food left, no hope remaining – climbed on to the battlements of the city one moonlit night.

The Mongols were all encamped around. The general could see them from the high walls. There was silence; there were the sleepers in the tents; there were the stars flung high above, and the general played on his pipe, played the most lonely, the most desolate melodies of the Steppes.

Soon after dawn, the enemy, now all utterly homesick,

departed. Remembering this I too play on my pipe for my daughter: Spaniard's Inn, Jack Straw's Castle, The Flask, The Everyman, The Screen on the Hill, Louis' Teashop, the Whitestone Pond and the donkeys, the *Ham and High*.

Another new, non-steroid, anti-inflammatory drug has been withdrawn as a result of the Committee on the Safety of Medicines turning their thumbs down. Three others over the last two years have met a similar fate.

This family of drugs is taken by hundreds of thousands of people in Britain. They have been prescribed widely in the main for arthritic pains of all varieties. One of them, Osmosin, as a matter of fact, was prescribed for my father-in-law by a hospital doctor in Lancashire.

Fortunately he suffered no ill effects. Others, less luckily, have experienced adverse reactions – some of them dire. There have been medical disasters such as gastro-intestinal perforations and blood dyscrasias. There have been mortalities.

Who is to blame? The greedy pharmaceutical companies or the gullible incautious, prescribing doctors? Both. There's no question that sometimes certain pharmaceutical firms, even in those advertisements they place in such prestigious periodicals as the *British Medical Journal*, make excessive claims for their drugs and print in the smallest type available the serious possible side-effects of these same drugs. Doctors read their advertisements and are influenced by them.

The *Lancet*, another journal which I read regularly with interest, quite justly has castigated doctors for often 'ignoring the hazards of a particular drug'. They further accuse doctors of being 'incapable of making a reasoned judgement' concerning the risks and benefits of this or that medicament.

The *Lancet* is right. Doctors have not the pharmacological expertise to make such judgements and that is why they so often have to accept the information doled out to them by so-called reputable drug companies.

Of course, many new drugs are wonderfully effective but not every physician remembers Alexander Pope's advice, 'Be not the first by whom the new are tried, Nor yet the last to lay the old aside.'

Doctors have always done harm as well as good. My favourite story of one who caused medical mayhem is told by the American doctor, Lewis Thomas, in his autobiography, *The Youngest Science*. He relates how a certain old-time physician, during the early years of this century, became extremely successful in New York, noted for his skill in making early diagnoses – especially of typhoid fever which was then a common disease in New York.

This great diagnostician, wrote Lewis Thomas, placed particular reliance on examining the tongue. 'He believed that he could detect significant differences by palpating that organ. The ward rounds conducted by this man were, essentially, tongue rounds; each patient would stick out his tongue while the eminence took it between thumb and forefinger, feeling its texture and irregularities, then moving from bed to bed, diagnosing typhoid in its earliest stages over and over again, and turning out a week or so later to have been right, to everyone's amazement.'

What we then learn from Lewis Thomas is that the old-time great diagnostician was, in fact, a typhoid carrier!

Driving home I heard on the radio that there is currently an epidemic of hip fractures in older people, especially in post-menopausal women. Such fractures, of course, are serious and it seems doctors are puzzled why, in recent years, there has been such a devastating increase in their incidence. 'You should see the orthopaedic wards of Nottingham hospitals. They are crowded with patients who have broken their hip bones. I'm not exaggerating.'

I listened to the experts offering hypotheses on why there is such an epidemic. Not enough Vitamin D in the diet, not enough calcium, failure of protein metabolism, etc., etc. Much talk of oestrogens and of bone conditions, osteomalacia and osteo-porosis. Concern, too, of the cost to the National Health Service.

I have news for these doctors. I recommend they turn their eyes from X-rays to look at the condition of our neglected towns. Let them get out of their cars and walk. Then they may observe the uneven state of the pavement stones here, there, everywhere, in the cities of run-down Britain.

April 1984

We all discover that certain 'facts' we learnt when young turn out to be no more than sweet myths or sour imaginings, born of pedagogic or parental pride and prejudice. Dai Smith, in his television programmes on BBC 2 and in his recently published book *Wales! Wales?* (Allen and Unwin) hatchets away at phoney national historiography.

I was taught at school, in Cardiff, about the particular, invented tradition of Wales, 'the Wales of symbols and gestures' of which Dai Smith speaks with love and astringency. As a result I still find it hard to separate Welsh myth from Welsh history, to erase the country in my mind that has been stencilled there by romantic didacticity and to replace it with the real Wales. I still feel, for instance, beyond reason and knowledge, that St David had two religions, one of these being rugby, and that somehow he, himself, was a useful scrum-half.

Even more bizarre notions have been passed on to me and have proved tenacious. Thus I believed my mother when she declared with passion that 'only common women wear green'. She was looking out of the front room window at a neighbour passing by. That must have been in 1937. I believed her then and I believed her a few years later, that time when Mair Jones lay down on the green grass in her green dress and said, 'Hello, you!'

I believed in my mother's colour prejudice in an undefined way until the mid 1960s when I happened to be passing Heals in Tottenham Court Road. Then, suddenly, a huge car purred to a standstill at the kerb near me. A chauffeur opened one of its doors and out stepped, not the Welsh rugby pack, but a lady dressed in green. She was Queen Elizabeth.

Next time I visited my mother in Cardiff I mentioned my so brief, royal, non-encounter. 'Yes,' my mother said, 'the Queen often wears green.' She nodded as if she were in the know. 'But you have views about women wearing green,' I said, surprised. It was my mother's turn to look surprised. 'How do you mean, son?' she asked.

*

While the Government is wasting one million pounds *a day* on the Falklands, Messrs Rees-Mogg and Luke Rittner who have been affectionately described by Bernard Levin as 'Butchers and Poulterers to the Gentry' have cut the Arts Council's already parsimonious *annual* Literature grant to £450,000. This particular exercise in butchery has hardly been commented on. Rather it has been the minor shifting of funds from London to the provinces that so far has drawn media attention. One could almost fancy this devolution of funds to be a tactic in order to disguise the real issues: lack of money for the Arts in general and for Literature in particular.

The Literature Panel of the Arts Council was strategically neutralised weeks before the Literature grant announcement. For it was leaked to Arts correspondents of certain newspapers that the Literature Panel was to be abolished. Now that it has been spared (temporarily?) its members are in disarray. Some like David Harsent and Catherine Freeman have resigned in despair. Others, such as Anne Stevenson and Tim Rix soldier on, illusorily hoping to fight some kind of last-ditch battle.

What power have the Arts Council's advisory panels? My own experience of sitting for three years on a past Literature Panel leads me to say, 'Damn all.' Minor suggestions were allowed and acted on but the real decisions were taken elsewhere. Then, as presumably now, one could in committee argue for this or that, against this or that, but often the debate was a masquerade. There is a Talmudic proverb that says it all: the stone fell on the pitcher? Woe to the pitcher. The pitcher fell on the stone? Woe to the pitcher.

Since my day on the Panel it seems the Arts Council's masters have become yet more active in creating an autocracy. Rees-Mogg really does appear to believe that, as in long centuries past, writers should have a private income. I do not know whether he and Luke Rittner are sensitive to the opinions of those in the field, I mean the writers themselves. Do the two gentlemen realise how much enmity they have engendered? At least the authors that I know, and with whom I have exchanged views, intemperately advocate sending them both to the bloody abattoir, and not as employees.

*

At a conference at the Royal College of Physicians, Dr Jack Dominian, consultant psychiatrist and Director of the Marriage Research Centre at the Central Middlesex Hospital, has produced statistics to prove that divorce increases the risk of mental and physical illness. He asserted that separated and divorced men and women suffer more minor psychiatric illness as well as being more prone to heart disease, road accidents and cirrhosis of the liver caused by drinking too much, than couples who adhere to married 'bliss and take'.

Surely Dr Dominian is wearing his trousers back to front? It seems more likely, does it not, that minor psychiatric illness leads to divorce rather than the other way around; that drinking too much leads to separation rather than being caused by it?

Perhaps Dr Dominian has statistics and arguments to prove the contrary; or has he been misreported in *The Times*? If not he should heed the story of the experimental biologist who placed a grasshopper on his research bench. The biologist shouted, 'Jump! Jump!' and measured the height that the insect reached. He repeated the exercise several times before he cut off the legs of the grasshopper.

After that amputation he again shouted, 'Jump! Jump!' Of course the grasshopper failed to respond to his commands. The biologist then concluded that when a grasshopper has its legs removed the insect loses its hearing.

Woe to the pitcher ... Michael Hamburger, I'm sure, would like that proverb because he, himself, has always affected a deep pessimism, as if all the apples on offer were made of wax, all the flowers on display made of paper. When we were both young and easy and hanging around Swiss Cottage I remember him saying that he did not expect to live long in this world. He shook his head mournfully as if he had just taken his own pulse.

One another occasion, at a small dinner party in our rather threadbare first floor flat in Eton Avenue, one of the guests, aged at least 24, remarked, 'I'm already losing hair here,' and he pointed to his growing widow's peak. 'So am I, man,' declared another guest, the American poet Theodore Roethke who, indeed, suffered from a somewhat profounder baldness. He looked across the table, ignoring the ladies. 'So am I,' I added.

Everybody now turned to Michael Hamburger who hesitated, then in a plaintive voice complained, 'I'm not. I wonder what's wrong with me?'

Now Michael Hamburger has recently celebrated his 60th birthday and he is being justly praised in the *Guardian* and elsewhere for his translations from the German and for his own considerable contribution to English Literature. But I expect he is still loudly moaning and groaning. 'Sixty,' I hear him languidly sigh, 'sixty, doctor, and none of my hair is falling out yet.'

After the Clinical Meeting we all sat for lunch, I myself next to a general practitioner. I have specialised in chest work and it is many years since I undertook a general practice locum in my home-town, Cardiff.

I still recall vividly my first morning surgery, my feelings of inadequacy. And later that afternoon when I went on my rounds, I had to hide my lack of confidence. My father insisted on being my chauffeur as I called on patients in Ruby Street or Stacey Road. He waited behind the wheel as I carried my little black bag into the patients' houses. When I returned to the waiting car he wanted to know in detail what the patient complained of and how I, his son, the doctor, had dealt with him or her. I had taken a helluva time to qualify so perhaps my father wanted to get his money's worth.

General practice has changed much since then. The GP next to me at lunch remarked how in his suburb, he now rarely makes house-calls. 'These days,' he reminded me, 'all the patients have cars. Besides there's the telephone.' I flinched. I recalled how the American doctor-essayist Lewis Thomas has justly pointed out that sick people usually need to be touched, that part of the problem of being ill is lack of human contact. Even family and friends tend to stay away from the profoundly ill. Moreover, medicine's technological advances have increased the distance between doctor and patient. After all, there was a time, before the discovery of the stethoscope, when physicians placed their ears on the patients' chests. Such a friendly gesture, such an 'intimate signal of personal concern and affection,' asserts Lewis Thomas.

My GP colleague picked at his salad. 'Yes,' he said, 'there have been some losses as well as immense gains.'

If the reviewers are to be believed the art of biography has reached dizzying heights. The nineteenth century critics were less kind. Thomas Carlyle remarked, 'A well-written Life is almost as rare as a well spent one.'

Nowadays, in the Sunday papers, one can regularly read rave reviews of X's *Life of Y*. For instance, the other Sunday, John Carey wrote that Ann Thwaite's biography of Edmund Gosse is 'one of the finest literary biographies of our time'. On my desk I have two other thick Lives to read: Richard Ellman's *James Joyce* which Anthony Burgess called 'the greatest literary biography of the century' – which may sound a bit MGM but I wouldn't mind such a review myself: and *Dostoevsky* by the remarkable Joseph Frank of which Bernard Levin writes, no doubt justly, that 'it's one of the outstanding biographical artistic works of modern times,' (Warner Brothers?).

I cannot imagine myself writing a biography. Think of all the research that has to be done, slowly, painstakingly! I haven't the scholar's patience of my wife, for instance, who a few years ago published a biography of John Ruskin, *The Passionate Moralist*, that also, incidentally, received MGM and Warner Bros reviews. Besides, I would have to silence, too drastically, the clamour that my own senses make, to annihilate self too much for too long a time. It is enough for me to lose myself constantly in my job as a doctor. For a doctor has to be inwardly quiet enough to hear the voice of his patient. He has to lose his own sense of self in order to make sense of a stranger.

Still, if I had to write a biography, if condemned to do so, whom would I choose? Thomas Hood, perhaps, – not only because I enjoy his work, his outrageous puns, but because, at least, I would know how to conclude the book. For Hood's last words to his wife were, punning to the end, 'My dear, I fear you're losing your livelihood.'

My eldest daughter Keren, went with some other women to Greenham Common last week. They were travelling down the

M4 in a packed car which had the CND emblem on the back. One of the girls joked, 'Perhaps the police will stop us – like they're stopping the miners.'

Half a mile later, the driver saw in the mirror a posse of policemen on motorbikes overtaking her. They resembled the ominous extras in Cocteau's film *Orphée*. The driver moved to the middle lane. Then, to all the women's consternation, they observed that the police were signalling them to move further over to the left.

Reluctantly, the car slowed to a stop on the hard shoulder. The police riding their motorbikes roared on. Then appeared several Rolls Royces tearing along in the same direction. In one was a visiting Arab potentate, the Amir of the State of Bahrein, who, presumably, had left Windsor Castle and was now on his way to visit the stables of the Queen at Highclere which is quite close to Greenham Common.

May 1984

I went for a morning walk on the beach at Ogmore-by-sea. The post-Easter blue skies still persisted and sunlight threw down its mercury-backed mirror dazzle on the sea. The beach was empty. I looked towards the barely-outlined coast of Somerset across the Bristol Channel and walked on, half-listening to the erratic rhythm of the sea.

Then, ahead of me, I saw a man, alone, sitting on the pebbles, his trousers tucked into his socks. Nearby lay a white stick. The man looked out, seemingly towards Somerset but, of course, he was blind. And I, walking on sand, and hence silently, suddenly felt myself to be a voyeur, watching him watch nothing.

I noticed how he was feeling the pebbles around him one by one. He picked them up, weighed them, felt, perhaps, the sun's faint warmth in them before replacing them, each one deliberately. He looked my way and seemed to smile so that I wondered, what parable is this? From behind a rock a woman now appeared, obviously his companion, and I strolled on listening once more to the sea and to the sorrowing of some seagulls.

*

That Saturday afternoon I went, for the last time this season, into Cardiff to watch The Bluebirds play at Ninian Park. Quitting the ground, I moved as quickly as possible back to my car. There was no crowd trouble on this occasion and I did not feel menaced as I have done earlier this year – because of running feet, because of a sudden stampede of rival supporters, because of raw shouts, over-alert policemen and police dogs barking.

These days, even approaching Saturday-afternoon football grounds has its suggestions of hazard. Not such a long time ago I used to enjoy the preliminaries to a football game. It began from the moment you locked the door of your car and some small boy would extend his hand saying, 'Mind it for sixpence, sir.' Afterwards you would join a stream of people, a benign stream that, in turn, would join another to form a river of supporters all flowing in the one imperative direction towards the mouth of the tall Stands.

Waiting there, and somehow contributing to the small excitements, would be the vendors wearing their white laboratory coats, selling rosettes, shiny programmes, ghastly onion-smothered sausages. And, in the ground itself, the dramatic crowds would be good-natured. Never would you hear, as I did at the Millwall ground recently, even before the game began, a whole mass of razor-headed young men shouting in unison, 'Kick their fuckin' 'eads in, kick their fuckin' 'eads in.' And brandishing their right fists rhythmically to this threatening cry, with routine malevolence.

Perhaps it is better that these lynch parties gather at football matches rather than elsewhere. To be sure these ranting, lead-irritable, broken-homed, frustrated, violent youths are a symptom of our unhealthy and increasingly uncaring society. But can football managerial staff attempt to undertake some palliative measures?

I was told by a Rumanian how they solved a crowd problem in Bucharest. Apparently the citizens of Bucharest are not given to queueing up. They have no discipline, the East Germans say. So, in their splendid football stands they would not sit in the seats numbered on the tickets that they had bought. Simply, they acted on the principle of first come, best seat. Then the faceless ones decided that at important games when the Stands were full a car would be given away to one particular occupant of a certain numbered seat. A kind of raffle. However if that occupant did not have the ticket with the right seat number the car was kept in the kitty, as it were, until the next big game. Soon the citizens of Bucharest became as obedient as East Germans.

Meanwhile lethal crowds or not, I still enjoy watching Cardiff City, the Bluebirds, play. I'm involved. I almost sing to myself. 'Roll along Cardiff City, roll along, to the top of the League where you belong. . . .' Some years back a friend lent me his season ticket to watch Spurs play. At White Hart Lane I had the pleasure of encountering Hans Keller or Professor Ayer. Refined company. Alas, that kind of bonus did not make up for not watching my home team. Despite the classy company, despite the classier football, I could not feel pure enthusiasm. I even felt the referee was fair!

Besides, the man who sat behind me had the habit of eating boiled sweets. Each time Spurs scored, one would be launched on the back of my head – a sticky orange, or raspberry, or lemon sweet would have to be pulled from my hair. I could tell how many goals Spurs had scored, including those disallowed, by the number of sweets I had to remove from the back of my neck. There are no such mad season ticket holders undergoing oral orgasms at Ninian Park. But then City don't score too many goals.

'I have writer's block,' the young man asserted, depressed. I knew the acute feeling of inertia he complained of. Most creative people have tasted the taste of nothing on the tongue. When writers feel this sense of deadness usually they are propelled to write something in order to prove to themselves that they are alive. Dylan Thomas, in his later thirties, suffered from writer's block. Each day arriving would feel to him to be purposeless and blank. So he would buy himself a Mars bar to keep for the morrow so that then he would have something to do, something to look forward to.

'How sad,' the young man said.

Sad, yes, but I cannot feel too sad these days for writers who experience this depressing inertia. There are too many unemployed. There are millions unable to face the new day creatively. How many of them feel as blank as a turned off TV screen? How many of them walk to the corner shop to buy a Mars bar? And how many attend a football game to run riot?

I did not say all this to my young friend. He did not need a lecture from me. I even resisted telling him the specific statistics that I learnt last weekend about 'unemployment-depression' in South Wales. In South and Mid-Glamorgan the number of suicides has increased over the last year by twenty-two per cent. More than half of those in Wales who attempt to kill themselves are unemployed. And those out of work for more than a year are nineteen times more likely to commit suicide than those with jobs.

'When I do manage to write a poem,' the young man said, 'may I show it to you?'

'I'd rather you didn't,' I said.

In our back garden in Golders Green, a host of golden dandelions! Or such was the case a couple of weeks ago. Now, though, the cherry blossom in wedding splendour floats its white petal confetti down to the rough grass and everywhere there are bluebells, bluebells, bluebells. I cannot help being reminded of Manley Hopkins who once remarked, 'I do not think I have ever seen anything more beautiful than the bluebell . . . I know the beauty of our Lord by it.'

One May, years ago, I had a visit from a Polish writer, Jerzy Sito, who has translated Shakespeare and Donne, as well as some modern British poets into his native language. Like Hopkins, he was enchanted by bluebells and told me – it still seems improbable – that there were no bluebells in Poland. He asked if he could take some to plant in his garden. Some years later he wrote that there were now active bluebells in Poland and all of them had come from our garden in Golders Green. I stick out my chest, swanky.

My father-in-law, Jack Mercer, who is still a vigorous 94 year old, offered us his new painting. He has been painting, as a hobby, since he retired and over the years he has given many of his pictures away to friends and relatives. Yet one Jack painted, over a decade ago, he keeps on the wall of his front room. It is a self-portrait, an idealised self-portrait. There he is, younger by far, looking somewhat like a blue-eyed film star. My father-in-law is and was a good looking fellow, but this self-portrait glamorizes him, erases the very defects which I think make his face more interesting.

If we could all paint self-portraits as competently as he, would we, too, artfully attempt to make ourselves somewhat more beautiful? After all, when it comes to photographs, the ones that flatter us a little, while remaining recognizably us, are the ones we like best! Mind you, all photographs, if we wait long enough, flatter us. Still, if I could paint adequately I don't think I would want a self-portrait on my wall. I would rather have hanging there some Maja on the balcony, some Virgin of the Rocks. Then with Ezra Pound perhaps I could whisper:

> The eyes of this dead lady speak to me.
> For here was love, was not to be drowned out.
> And here desire, not to be kissed away.

How much do portraits reveal a man's or a woman's character? Hazlitt believed that a man's life may be a lie to himself and to others but 'a picture of him painted by a great artist would probably stamp his true character on the canvas and betray the secret to posterity'.

I hope Hazlitt was wrong. Some years back Josef Herman painted a powerful portrait of me. He sold it to the gallery of the Welsh National Museum and when my mother went to have a look at it there – she was then in her eighties – she made an embarrassing fuss. 'That's not my son,' she apparently said to everybody within megaphone distance, 'that looks like the devil.' They finally had to call the curator. Meanwhile she stared at the nearby idealised painting of Dylan Thomas by Augustus John, all curly hair, all soulful eyes. My mother seethed. No wonder, soon after, Josef Herman's portrait was removed to the darkness of the Museum's store room. As my mother said, 'Now, if Jack had painted you, you would have looked as nice as Dylan Thomas.'

Robert Edwards and Patrick Steptoe, the 'test-tube baby' pioneers, based at Bourn Hall, Cambridge, have stressed the obstetrical and social risks involved in promoting multiple pregnancies and have criticised the Hammersmith Hospital team under Mr Robert Winston, who implanted six embryos in the uterus of a certain Mrs Janice Smale with the result that this lady gave birth to quads. (The other two fertilized eggs did not develop.) Robert Winston has responded angrily, 'We do not carry out research on embryos or freeze them for later use as they do at Bourn Hall.'

Bob Edwards is the most audacious scientist I have ever met and one who, since a boy, has been almost obsessively interested in pregnancy, animal and human. I recall with what enthusiasm he once told me how the beginnings of life have never failed to fascinate him. He was thrilled when he first observed the human embryos he had incubated divide into two cells, into four cells, into eight cells, each cell with its own nucleus. It was the beauty of the embryo's growth, the way it became magnificently organised, how it switched on its own biochemistry, and increased its size and prepared itself for implantation in the womb that excited him.

More than that: how the embryo's organs form, the cells gradually becoming capable of developing into heart and lung, brain and eye. 'What a unique and wonderful process it is,' he said, 'as the increasing number of cells diverge and specialize in a delicate, integrated and coordinated manner. One day all the secrets of this early development may be known and those same secrets may help us to repair the ravages and defects in the tissues of sick and ageing men and women.'

Bob Edwards is a man with a bold vision. And Patrick Steptoe, too, is no slouch when it comes to responsible medical adventuring. So when these two men grumble about others going too far, I feel instinctively we should be alerted. But Mr Robert Winston, too, in his reponses, has made statements to which we should pay close attention. He has written in the *Observer* that the standards of infertility treatment in this country are scandalously poor. He makes the shocking accusation that 'Women are given drugs to ovulate when they ovulate already; much tubal surgery is performed with instruments more suitable for sharpening pencils. . . .' Such serious charges should be considered seriously and the public not diverted into wondering instead about the ethical dimensions of freezing embryos.

Not that the practice of freezing embryos is one to be ignored. Already there is a tiny baby in Australia who less than a year ago was but a frozen embryo. In the same Melbourne Hospital where that baby was born there are, it seems, hundreds of other embryos in suspended animation.

Already, in the eighteenth century, the remarkable Dr John Hunter imagined that, 'it might be possible to prolong life to any period by freezing a person in the frigid zone as I thought all action and waste would cease until the body thawed. I thought that if a man could give up the last years of his life to this kind of alternative oblivion and action, it might be prolonged to a thousand years; and by getting himself thawed every hundred years he might learn what had happened during his frozen condition. . . .'

Hunter took two living carp and froze them in river water. When he eventually thawed them out the fish were dead, dead as fish fingers! The embryological researches carried out at Bourn Hall and all over our 1984 world are likely to be much more successful. No wonder scientists and doctors such as Bob Edwards and Robert Winston await guidance from the Warlock Committee who report to the Government in June about the legal, ethical and social implications of 'test-tube' fertilization and embryo research.

I put on an old sports jacket I had not worn for years. In one of its pockets I found an envelope on the back of which I had written: 'I'm never at home in a garden; I'm always a visitor.' I quite like that, but did I make it up myself or did I copy it from some book I had read? I don't remember.

I am a sucker for aphoristic sayings. I love wisdom stories, parables, proverbs. Many seem to stick in my head. When I was a student I stayed in a boarding house which had a card on the wall. It read: 'If you have two pennies to spend, spend one penny on bread that you may live; spend the other on a flower that you may have a reason for living.' This was purported to be an Old Chinese saying and is, I realize now, rather twee. But I liked it at the time and it has stayed with me.

Then there's the old Zen saying I came across about the same time and which I'm still not ashamed to know and quote: 'To a man who knows nothing, mountains are mountains, waters are waters and trees are trees. But when he has studied and knows a little, mountains are no longer mountains, waters no longer waters, and trees no longer trees. But when he has thoroughly understood, mountains are once again mountains, waters are waters and trees are trees.'

Some 'wise' sayings stay with me from the days when I was a medical student. For instance, there's Pliny's complaint that the Greek physician was the 'only person who could kill another with sovereign impunity' or the dictum of a certain twentieth century London consultant that 'the anus is the sentinel of social security'.

Parables? Here's one I learnt through Martin Buber of the Baal-Shem that particularly appeals to me: 'Once some musicians stood and played, and a great group moved in dance in accordance with the voice of the music. Then a deaf man came there who knew nothing of music and dancing and thought in his heart, 'How foolish these men are: some beat with their fingers on all kinds of implements and others turn themselves this way and that.'

I wish somebody would edit an Oxford Book of Parables and Wisdom Sayings. I would be the first to buy a copy. I hope such an editor would sensibly include in it wry Yiddish jokes for some, in fact, are very close to being proverbs. Take, for example, that modern definition of a psychiatrist: 'A Jewish doctor who hates the sight of blood.' Or better still that older one: 'If the rich could hire other people to die for them the poor would make a wonderful living.' I wonder what shadowy, bearded figure dressed in ridiculous black, walking somewhere in Latvia or Lithuania, Poland or Russia, suddenly pulled out his pencil and, inspired and feelingly, wrote that down on the back of an envelope?

June 1984

I was asked to participate some years ago in a pilot programme for a projected TV series entitled *Friends of John Betjeman*. I hardly knew Sir John so was surprised by the invitation. However, I enjoyed his poems and looked forward to spending a day with him at the London Weekend Studios.

Over a lively lunch John Betjeman told me he would begin the programme with Thomas Hood's poem, 'I remember, I remember, the house where I was born.' He continued, 'Some may think it sentimental but it isn't, it isn't, and I don't care if it is.' After Hood's poem, the Poet Laureate then intended to air his enthusiasm for other poets including Edward Thomas. He would request Prunella Scales to read Thomas's 'Adelstrop'. 'At this point you come into it,' he advised me. 'We'll talk about Edward Thomas before I ask you to read your poem, 'Not Adelstrop,' all right?'

Before we went into the studio I asked if he, Sir John, had been influenced by Thomas Hood, by, for instance, the rhythms of 'The Bridge of Sighs'. Sir John gave me a dazzling smile before opening his eyes wide to recite by heart the whole of 'The Bridge of Sighs'. Hearing that poem mediated through his voice Hood sounded utterly Betjemanesque:

> In she plunged boldly
> No matter how coldly
> The rough river ran.
> Over the brink of it
> Picture it – think of it
> Dissolute man!. . .
>
> Take her up tenderly
> Lift her with care
> Fashioned so slenderly
> Young and so fair.

Soon after, we sat in the harsh TV lights – Sir John, Prunella Scales and I – for a rehearsal. His illness had left him in decline and though he could recite Thomas Hood at length, and accurately, he displayed memory lapses which agitated the producer. The latter began to wonder whether Sir John was now capable of performing as 'an anchor man' for the seven programmes planned. Prunella Scales, who was accustomed to working with Sir John Betjeman, whispered, 'Don't worry, he's always like this at rehearsal. When we actually do it, he'll be brilliant, you'll see.'

During the actual performance before a studio audience Sir John, alas, did lose his place and did bumble rather. He forgot to mention Edward Thomas so I had to ask him, 'Do you like Edward Thomas, his poem 'Adelstrop' for instance?' I did not think these promptings mattered too much. Soon he was asking Prunella Scales to read Thomas's poem and his hesitations, his transparent recoveries, his now obvious vulnerability, surely made him all the more likeable to a viewing audience? Certainly the studio audience warmed to him.

The producer, though, felt the programme was not smooth and professional enough. So the series was cancelled and this pilot programme not shown. I wish they would find a slot for an edited version of it now. Viewers do not want mere slick professionalism and would surely respond to his enthusiasm and to his hesitating, friendly unpredictability.

After that pilot programme many of the studio audience approached Sir John with books to be signed. Books by John Betjeman piled up in front of him. It so happened that on the table lay my own *Collected Poems* from which I had read earlier. John Betjeman, signing book after book, accidentally wrote his signature in mine. Thus I can proudly boast that, in my bookcase, I now have my *Collected Poems* signed by John Betjeman. That should fool one or two collectors!

Dr Billy Graham has long been described as a particularly charismatic evangelist. It was cold that recent May day in Sunderland, when he preached to the 16,000 crowd in the football stadium at Roker Park. Whatever else charisma does for you, it does not keep you warm. 'It's the coldest open air weather I've ever preached in,' Dr Graham complained. He admitted to wearing two pairs of thermal underwear. When you come down from the mountain should you feel so cold?

We use the term 'charisma' nowadays to signify a magical,

appealing power that certain individuals emanate. Successful prophets have it, messiahs trade on it, fringe healers depend on it, politicians long for it, evangelists such as Dr Graham (they say) exude it. Such charismatic characters, it would appear, are capable of generating a collective excitement among those who spiritually surrender to them.

Psychoanalysts tell us that we all possess a vestigial longing to discover a god-like personage with unlimited power and wisdom. When we were children we believed our parents to be omniscient and omnipotent. The child is father of the man and our longing to discover our parents as they once seemed to be, becomes more pronounced when we feel defeated and helpless. Then we are most open to the hypnotic power of a seemingly caring charismatic figure who, we irrationally hope, can solve our problems and our ills. Such a figure may be both father and mother to us. Father-like, authoritatively, he will tell us what we must do and simultaneously, mother-like, he will comfort us, be infinitely sympathetic.

The hypnotist works like that. 'Raise your right arm,' he commands us with masculine sternness. Then in a darkened room, stroking us gently, softening his voice to a lullaby, mother-like, he tells us, 'You're sleepy now, child, very sleepy.'

The psychoanalysts' view that charismatic leaders are able to project both the masculine and feminine components of their personality like hypnotists, seems to me to be plausible. Take Mrs Thatcher, for instance. There are those, a considerable number, who do not believe her to be The Great British Disaster. On the contrary, be they Cabinet subservient or troubled Mrs Smith, our neighbour, they find in her the bossy masculine prototype, our stern Daddy, and, at the same time, when she turns her feminine side towards them, our dear, sweet Mum. In short, just what the patient ordered.

But to get back to Dr William Graham. What I want to know is – what does wearing two sets of thermal underwear do for your charisma?

My favourite religious charismatic was one who lived in twelfth century Yemen. (His name escapes me.) When he proclaimed himself to be the Messiah he was hauled in chains before the

King who himself was a lineal descendant of Fatima, the Prophet's daughter. The King, a doubting man evidently, invited the chained fanatic to prove his credentials.

'Maybe perform some miracle?' suggested the King.

The aspiring messiah agreed. 'Cut off my head,' he urged the King confidently. 'Then I'll return to life again.'

The King obliged the charismatic and subsequently, with growing disappointment, waited patiently for the miracle that did not take place.

That cold day in May when Billy Graham wore his two pairs of knickers I leaned over the railings of the lower pond in Golders Hill Park watching the Australian white swan with the black neck. It hardly moved, remaining there in concussed reverie. It was late, almost closing time, and the Park had emptied.

I walked up and around in a horizontal arc towards the main gate. Then I observed, in front of me, a figure sprawled on a wooden bench, swathed in cloth, an old balaclava about his head, a scarf up to his nostrils. If I had been a child I would have known, without a doubt, that here, now, that May evening, I had encountered the primal Bogeyman!

Being an adult, I merely looked around uneasily for other human company. No one else was about. I approached, his eyes were shut and I thought how the night dreams of the sane and of the insane are little different from each other. He did not move and I began to wonder if he were dead. For a moment I watched him as I had the swan earlier. Both so motionless. Then, to my relief, the inert figure stirred and I passed on, leaving the tramp, if tramp he was, to his own dreamings. As I left the park the lamps in West Heath Drive lit up and the earliest dark flowed through the railings; and I wondered if the Bogeyman would stay on that bench all night. Poor old fella.

It is not every day that one's son gets married. Disliking formality, I had not at first been overjoyed when he and his bride, Sue Morris, decided they wanted a religious ceremony followed by a real reception. Weddings, I believed, should be observed quietly. Besides, it meant me wearing my one suit which is a bit hot for

June. In the event, the ceremony was touchingly beautiful and the reception an occasion of much pleasure. All the same I was somewhat taken aback that I received so many requests *not* to make a speech.

Perhaps some present recalled that, once upon a time when I was sour sixteen, I took part in a school debate in which I advocated that the Institution of Marriage was Bankrupt. I have, after my own experience, changed my mind. Balzac, surely, was utterly sensible when he declared that it is as absurd to say that a man can't love one woman all the time as it is to say that a violinist needs several violins to play the same piece of music.

It is a long time (1951) since the *Ham and High* wickedly announced our fugitive wedding. 'Dannie Abse of 50 Belsize Square', the hound reported, 'married Joan Mercer of 50 Belsize Square at Hampstead Registry Office'. Afterwards Joan and I went off to the Blue Danube Club in Swiss Cottage with a few of our slightly drunk friends. It was a really nice occasion: I'm just sorry my son and his bride could not have been there.

I live a guarded life. I rarely have to embark on the intrepid adventure of shopping. On Thursday, though, I needed to post a parcel to the USA and I discovered I had no money on me. 'I'll just pop into the bank,' I told my wife. 'I won't be long'. She then, unusually, asked me to do some shopping for her at Sainsbury's. 'Just a few items,' she reassured me.

So off I went on my great mission, first to Barclays Bank, then to Golders Green Post Office, then to Sainsbury's. As I walked down Rodborough Road the sun shone down on the débris from MacDonalds that had thoughtfully been shoved at happy intervals in the green hedges of front gardens. Seeing me with shopping bag the birds whistled in the trees, delighted.

At Barclays Bank I waited in a morose queue. Nobody smiled. I waited and waited. Eventually I cashed my cheque and left the reverent hushed atmosphere of the bank for the noise of Finchley Road. I walked the length of a cricket pitch before reaching Golders Green Post Office where the queue stretched almost to the door and looked even more depressed. So much so that I felt everybody urgently needed a dose of electro-convulsive therapy. I waited and I waited and I waited. At last I reached the grid where a reasonably civil, civil servant picked up my parcel very slowly. I took my own pulse.

Later I crossed the road to the emporium of Sainsbury's where I cleverly selected the items my wife required, then found I had to join an impossible queue to pay for them. I waited and I waited and I waited and I waited. In Sainsbury's one has to be more patient than a patient. No wonder a row began. Some gent devoid of his motorcar had pushed an old lady aside and a strenuous young woman bottled up with just feminist ardour went into battle against this masculine swine. I agreed with her, but some minutes later I was prepared to certify several members of the queue, especially those ahead of me.

By the time I returned to the safety of my own house the best part of the morning had gone. My wife did not ask me why I had taken so long to do so little. Like a child I suggested simplistically that Barclays Bank, the Post Office, Sainsbury's, etc. should employ more people and give us all a better service. 'Vote to reduce queues,' I said, 'including those in the Job Centres.' 'Isn't it the head man at Sainsbury's whose advice the Prime Minister is going to take about the reorganization of the National Health Service?' my wife asked.

Drug addiction in Britain is a growing problem. That I knew; but I was surprised when I learnt how often the drug addict turns out to be the favourite son of a family. Common to many a drug addict, apparently, is an over-close relationship with his mother. From case histories it is evident that not infrequently the mother of the drug addict has no husband – he may have taken off or died years earlier. Thus the widow or grass widow feels all the more need to be needed by her son who develops, as it were, into a surrogate husband.

If such are the satisfactions of a number of such mothers what are those of their sons? Experts testify how patients tell them quite directly that 'the works' as they call it in the argot, (that is to say, the syringe and needle), is like a breast. 'When the addict is high', Dr Isidore Chein has written, 'he feels that he is together with his mother, long ago, warm, comfortable, happy, at peace; when he injects the opiate solution, he mixes the solution with his blood and bounces the blood-opiate mixture back and forth from syringe to vein and, as he does this, he has fantasies of intercourse.'

Such testimonies may seem outlandish, even repugnant to some. Yet only through such interpretations can the addict's description of a fix be understood. Alexander Trocchi, the Scottish novelist who died recently was an addict and he wrote in *Cain's Book*: 'When one presses the bulb of the eye-dropper and watches the pale, blood-streaked liquid disappear through the nozzle and into the needle and the vein it is not, not only, a question of feeling good. It's not only a question of kicks. The ritual itself, the powder in the spoon, the little ball of cotton, the matches applied, the bubbling liquid drawn up through the cotton filter into the eye-dropper, the tie round the arm to make a vein stand out, the fix often slow because a man will stand there with the needle in the vein and allow the level in the eye-dropper to waver up and down, up and down, until there is more blood than heroin in the dropper – all this is not for nothing: it is born of a respect for the whole chemistry of alienation. When a man fixes he is turned on almost instantaneously . . . you can speak of a flash, a tinily murmured orgasm in the bloodstream, in the central nervous system.'

Trocchi was glamorizing something sad and shabby and sick and I doubt if he understood fully the symbolic significance of what he was saying.

Near the gates, East and West, of Golders Hill Park, tables had been set up. On these, petition forms were available for people to sign and protest against the possible abolition of the GLC. 7416 men and women signed the petition and the forms have now been forwarded to Sir Geoffrey Finsburg, Hampstead's MP. These figures have come my way because Mr F. G. Taylor, who works in the park, has a small, friendly quarrel with me.

For, some months ago, I suggested that attractive Golders Hill is not widely known. To prove I was wrong Mr Taylor 'analysed' the addresses of 3000 of those who signed the petition. Many indeed came from afar. The addresses were located in 60 London postal districts and 23 English counties. Some came from even further outposts of Britain.

Yet one I saw last month in the failing evening light, just before the Park closed, I bet had no address. I was going home towards the West gate when I saw him sprawled on the wooden bench. He was swathed in cloth, an old balaclava about his head, a scarf up to his nostrils. If I had been a child, I would have known without a doubt that this motionless figure was no other than the primal Bogeyman himself. As an adult, I was only fifty per cent sure. That's why, uneasy, still I wish Mr Taylor would go through the other 4416 signatures just to see if Mr Bogeyman left his autograph there.

July 1984

A Canterbury Tale Chaucer did not write concerns a consultant surgeon, Mr M. R. Williams FRCS, who allowed his friend, the vet, to assist him during a hernia operation at a local hospital. Mr Williams, who used to teach medical students at St Thomas's Hospital, apparently allowed the vet to make the initial incision and to stitch up afterwards. All this, of course, under his supervision, but the newspapers have reported, 'This revelation has caused serious concern to a shocked medical profession.'

I can imagine the placards in Canterbury: LOCAL VET SHOCK. It is no joke, though, for Mr Williams, already the cemetery side of sixty, has had his retirement date brought forward. I can imagine, too, the patient who, now fully recovered, no doubt pulls up his shirt, lowers his trousers, and boasts, 'Hey, hey, look at this scar. This is what the vet did.'

When I was in South Wales last week it was warm enough to go swimming. And I did – into the dirty waves of Ogmore-by-sea. Afterwards I had a cup of tea with my friend, Roger Palmer, who works for an air-conditioning firm. The economy in Wales, of course, as everybody knows, is particularly depressed. So one does not ask anyone, 'How's business?' I'm reminded of an old Jewish joke. Mr Cohen complains to Mr Goldstein, 'Goldstein, you never ask me how business is these days.' Goldstein shrugs his shoulders and asks, 'Well, how's business?' Mr Cohen rolls his eyes. 'Don't ask,' he replies.

But Roger Palmer told me *voluntarily* how his firm was doing.

'Business is booming,' he said. 'Fantastic.' I was surprised. That day it was quite hot, but all said and done, South Wales is hardly the South of France. I looked up at the sky. To have air-conditioning put into your villa or slum in Glamorgan does seem somewhat epicurean.

'Oh, it's not for people for the most part,' Roger said scornfully. 'It's for computers.'

I was puzzled until I learnt that computers do not like sticky, muggy weather. So where people work, where they have worked for years, in sometimes muggy conditions, now there stands, or rather sits, a beautiful, spoilt machine. For computers, it seems, are more refined than human beings. They'll go on strike at the hint of thunder. So the air-conditioning business thrives.

Mr Keating telephoned to ask if he could visit me. 'I'm doing a thesis,' he explained. What a sensible fellow, I thought, to under-take a thesis on *my* work. I warmed to him at once. I would help him. However, I soon gathered that he wanted to interview me only because he had begun writing a thesis on Stevie Smith!

'I would be obliged,' he said, 'if you would give me your impressions of her as a person. I know you shared a platform with Stevie Smith on various occasions. I once heard you both at the Theatre Royal in Stratford East.'

He had heard us *both*, I pondered, and wanted to write a thesis on *Stevie*. I cooled towards the fellow in an instant. I claimed, truthfully, little acquaintance with Stevie Smith, but Mr Keating was insistent. Reluctantly I agreed to see him.

I would tell him about another telephone call I had once received that led to my one and only altercation with Stevie Smith. It was from David Carver, the then Secretary of the PEN, who wanted my opinion about the current standing of Robin Skelton's reputation, who, visiting London from Canada, had offered to give a poetry reading for PEN. David Carver had, in any case, it seemed, intended to sponsor a PEN reading some time at the Porchester Hall and was, indeed, on the look-out for an important poet-reader.

'Would Skelton attract a large enough audience?' asked Mr Carver. 'Do you think it would be better if I asked someone like Stevie Smith instead?'

'Why not both of them?' I suggested.

I knew that Stevie would draw an audience. During the last few years she had become popular partly because of the Poetry and Jazz readings arranged by Jeremy Robson. Stevie was considerably older than the other poets who shared that platform with her. She was almost 70 and looked like a very thin great-aunt about to say 'Don't'. Perhaps the audience had expected, from her appearance, to hear dull hymns to Flowers, Elves and Bees. At first they viewed her with suspicion but soon she was reciting:

> I was much too far out all my life
> And not waving but drowning.

Or surprisingly, she would sing her lines excruciatingly, daringly, off-key. The audience warmed to her, cheered her audacity.

Later David Carver telephoned to say that Stevie wanted to read solo. She had declared that she *never* read with anyone else!

'Nonsense,' I said. 'I'll persuade her if you like.'

Most poets prefer not to read in tandem but usually agree to do so if pressed. And if Robin Skelton wanted to read, well, why not?

My telephone call to Stevie was a disaster. She was harsh, regally adamant. She did not sound like the Stevie Smith I knew. She seemed to be invaded by some alien personality, one I had never met and I put down the telephone, upset, defeated. So Stevie Smith read at the Porchester Hall, solo. I did not attend her reading.

Some months later I met her at a party and, happily, we became 'friends' again. That was the last time I saw Stevie for, soon after, she became ill, suffering from a brain tumour. In retrospect, I wonder whether her apparent personality change, her uncharacteristic response to my telephone call, was an early sign of her lesion. Probably not. In any case, I can hardly imagine how such a surmise can help Mr Keating one way or another.

The man at the bar took the pipe out of his mouth and said to Vernon Scannell, 'Since you're a poet you should know where this comes from.' Then he proudly recited, 'Loveliest of trees. . .' Vernon interrupted him with, 'Housman'. The man narrowed his eyes. 'Look,' he said, 'if you can tell me who wrote this I'll buy you a pint.' He recited more Housman and Vernon Scannell replied, 'A. E. Housman.' The pint glass was soon emptied. 'I'll buy you another one,' said the pipe-smoking gentleman reciter of poetry, 'if you guess who the author is this time.'

He intoned more lines of verse and yet again Vernon Scannell interrupted him with a triumphant, 'Housman.' The quiz continued, the prize always being a pint. However, the man who wanted to recite poetry and confound Vernon Scannell knew only the work of Housman. He kept on reciting his favourite poet and as Vernon called out Housman, each time less clearly, pints were bought for all. Just before closing time, though, I don't think Vernon heard what lines were being recited, yet clever as Dick, he mumbled, 'Housman.' And the man was amazed at Vernon's extraordinary erudition.

It always surprises me how many people, given half a chance, will with evident pleasure recite the verses they know off by heart. My own mother, after a couple of wine gums, could be persuaded, drear of tone and wild of eye, to recite 'Hiawatha' – the whole of it. Once my mother got going she was hard to stop. 'O the famine and the fever!' she would howl. 'O the wailing of the children!'

There used to be an annual Festival of Spoken Poetry. It went on successfully for some thirty years until 1959. The winner that last year was a beautiful young lady named Betty Mulcahy. Not long ago I happened to hear Ms Mulcahy read out loud, at a concert, a poem by Vernon Scannell. The poem, a striking one, was called 'Taken in Adultery'. The Master of Ceremonies who introduced the reading did so without punctuation. Breathlessly he said, 'Betty Mulcahy, taken in adultery by Vernon Scannell.' That made a few people raise their eyebrows.

Tomorrow (July 21st) at the Guildhall School of Music Theatre, the Festival of Spoken Poetry is being revived as part of the City of London Festival. One of the judges is, most appropriately, Betty Mulcahy and now the winner of this Speak a Poem event will win a prize of £1000. Yes, £1000. I wonder if that pipe-smoking Housman fan will be one of the entrants.

*

I understand that recently some 1.4 million Americans have been in London. I should think that figure is correct because I reckon 1.2 million of them have called on me. One of my favourite visitors told me how many of his compatriots in New Orleans have a high regard for French culture – that if they weren't Americans they would like to have been French. I thought of the Frenchman who once told the Duke of Wellington, 'If I wasn't French I should have liked to have been English.' 'If *I* wasn't English,' the Iron Duke apparently replied, 'I would like to have been English.'

For years I've been grumbling about British Rail. Not so long ago I used to take my father-in-law to Euston Station for his return journey to Lancashire. I never had to worry about finding him an empty seat. It was, because of the extortionate railway prices, a question of him choosing which empty *carriage* he preferred. I would stand on the platform watching the long, almost empty, train pull away and think, 'When I get home I'll write a crisp letter to Peter Parker saying, *'Why don't you lower the fares?'* I never did, of course.

Several years later some fantastic genius working for BR had the happy idea that the trains might be used a bit if fares were reduced. And so they have been, despite the intricacy of the Saver Fares – those concessions of Byzantine complexity that any fool who possesses the wisdom of Solomon and the patience of Griselda can easily work out.

Last week I caught, or meant to catch, the 3 p.m. train to Liverpool. At Euston I extracted £17 from my pocket, having no Persil boxes on me and asked for the Inter City Saver. 'No Inter City fares after 3 p.m.,' said the clerk victoriously. I was puzzled; last time I bought a ticket Inter City fares were finished after 4 p.m. 'Yes,' said the clerk, 'that used to be so. Now it's 3 p.m.

Then I remembered the train left at 3 p.m. so I said, 'Well, the train, in any case, leaves at 3 p.m. so surely I can have an Inter City fare?' The clerk was now almost on the verge of laughter. 'That train used to be at 3 p.m.,' he said, 'but they've changed it to 3.05 p.m. Your timetable is, ha, out of date.' Now came the biggest joke of all. 'The fare is £41.50,' the clerk added with purest joy.

I was not going to pay £41 bleeding 50. I turned angrily away. I'll write a letter, I thought. I'll write a letter to BR asking whether those people employed only to change timetables might be given a little rest *at the nearest bloody mental hospital*. Gradually my anger subsided. I *had* to go to Liverpool so there was no choice. I turned back to the ticket office, ready to capitulate. Now, though, a queue had formed. I waited, but I think somebody ahead of me was also having trouble with the arcane secrets of the Fare Structure. If I loitered any longer I would miss the 3 p.m. train, I mean the 3.05 p.m. train, thank heavens. So I raced past the barrier like Steve Ovett, having decided that I would have to pay on the train.

Eventually the ticket collector appeared. I asked for an Inter-City ticket. '£17, sir,' he said. 'What a nice fellow', I thought. 'What a nice, ignorant fellow'. After I had given him the money he sweetly departed and I opened the newspaper that I had brought with me. At once, a huge BR advertisement caught my eye: PROSPECTS FOR THE RAILWAY CUSTOMER LOOK MUCH BETTER.

Inspiration. What is its nature, what does it mean? One dictionary states that it is an 'influence of the Spirit of God upon the human mind or soul.' Scriptural writers may well have received divine assistance in preparing their texts but what about us secular lot?

I have always liked Pasteur's words on scientific inspiration – 'Chance favours the prepared mind,' he remarked. I like, too, a story I heard recently about a champion golfer who, obviously inspired, holed in one. 'What luck,' cried one bystander. The golfer nodded. 'You're right,' he said. 'And the odd thing is that the more I practise the luckier I get.'

August 1984

The dream was continuously black and white. I can only remember the corybantic rags of it and what I do recall is absurd – as if Margaret Thatcher appeared on stage in classical ballet dress with coal dust on her face and wearing a CND badge. Dreams often are ridiculous. Didn't Freud once say, 'Dreams are most profound when they seem most crazy'? But then he believed, like the prophets and kings of old, that a dream uninterpreted was like a letter unread.

Some dreams stay with us all our lives though they may be uncoloured and far from spectacular. For instance, I remember one dream from thirty-five years ago. A bird alighted on my shoulder, stayed on my shoulder. Because of this feathered creature I was followed by a horde of cats who, in turn, were followed by a procession of dogs. There is more to my dream than that, several disjointed scenes, but I won't elaborate. I do not wish to bore you. For our dreams, generally, while fascinating to ourselves, usually bore others.

Other people's nightmares are a little more interesting perhaps than their milder dreams – such as the one John Ruskin recorded in his diary and commented on as being the ghastliest nightmare of his life. Ruskin in his oneiric trance observed an old dying surgeon dissecting himself. 'It was worse than dissecting – *tearing*,' wrote Ruskin on December 27th, 1875, 'and with circumstances of horror about the treatment of the head which I will not enter.' Ruskin's castration anxieties often seemed to guide the speedless direction and normal delirium of his dreams. He himself sometimes attributed his horror-film night visions to a lamb chop or some other item of food he had too much enjoyed the previous evening.

The patient had the same name as me: Abse. He was a Lebanese Christian. 'Is Abse a common name in the Middle East?' I asked. Unsmiling, he nodded and told me he had encountered the name in Egypt and Syria as well as in the Lebanon. 'It's an old name,' he said. 'Have you heard of the poet, Abse?' Taken aback, I hesitated. 'The great poet, Abse,' he added. This is my day, I thought, but he continued, 'The great poet, Abse, who lived in the sixth century, at the time of the prophet.'

I swallowed. I looked at him suspiciously. But it was quite evident that he did not know that I too scribbled away, scribble, scribble, scribble. 'The great poet, Antara el Abse,' Mr Abse said. 'I'm not a literary man but Antara is famous among Arabs. He was a robber-prince and was half-black.'

Later I learned from reading an essay by Bernard Lewis in an old *Encounter* that the blacks had been persecuted in the Moslem sixth century world. No wonder Antara wrote:

> Half of me comes from the family of Abse,
> The other half I defend with my sword.

I like that. I wouldn't mind sticking those two lines at the top of my notepaper. Indeed, the more I hear of this Antara el Abse the more I'm willing to claim him as a long-lost ancestor.

Once, it seems, a crowd shrank before a huge wild bull. One man cried to Antara, 'Only Antara can deal with that bull.' Antara el Abse nodded in seeming agreement, then answered, 'Ye-es, but does that bull know I'm Antara?'

The Italian waiter was, you might say, operatic. He ignored our earnest conversation about the miners' sorry predicament and the Government's expensive inflexibility and sang a Verdi phrase or two as he served us. At the next table, the lady, smiling, asked for the bill. He presented it to her as though it were a bouquet of roses. She said, putting on her glasses, 'Does this include service?' He almost pirouetted. 'Yes, madam,' he said, 'it includes service, but not the tip.'

My companions discussed Goethe's dying words, 'Mehr licht.' One of them wondered whether Goethe, in pronouncing his 'More light' was merely requesting greater illumination in order that he might see more clearly the beautiful face of the woman at his bedside. Another, more religiously inclined, suggested that he was trying to tell those in attendance something about the nature of heaven whose gates he was at. After all, there is a legend that in the world to come the light of the moon shall be as the light of the sun and the light of the sun shall be sevenfold.

Why do Last Words interest us at all? Why do they seem more important than say, the utterances of a man or woman on the occasion of a 40th birthday? Do we assume that only at the end of life can a lifetime's vision be summarized in one pithy sentence, be whispered, like a secret, to the near and dear ones at the bedside? Or do we believe that a man faced with death will reveal himself as never before, not wishing in that solemn hour to deceive anyone?

More likely our curiosity springs from the childish belief that a man or woman at Death's portals is well-placed to tell us something of the terrain from which no traveller returns and for which we are, alas, all eventually bound. We who are tourists not yet set out, listen fearfully to a tourist who has almost awesomely arrived.

The fact is, though, that those recorded words of the dying are almost always falsified or just simply manufactured. Goethe, for instance, did not actually whisper, 'Mehr licht.' Instead, he softly requested, 'Open the second shutter so that more light can come in.' But how much more memorable is the fictive, ambiguous, 'More Light.' If Goethe had lived to record his own dying words they would doubtless have been more memorable still!

Spike Milligan once asked me if I knew Gladstone's Dying Words. I shook my head. Putting on a Spike Milligan funny voice Spike Milligan uttered, 'I feel better now.' Perhaps Gladstone did actually expire with those words. For surely the more banal the saying the more likely it is to be true. I do not believe Beethoven's spooky and striking, 'I shall hear in heaven.' I do believe King George V's 'How is the Empire?'

Yesterday I went in search of a haircut. I had put off visiting a barber because . . . well, who over 40 years of age enjoys visiting a hairdresser?

Each time you submit to the snip snip snip of a triumphant pair of scissors you observe how the hair clinging to the front of the white gown has become more silvery and aged. As if that were not defeating enough, they make you face a mirror, a huge, tactless, devil-mirror. And when the snip snip snip is over they, cockily, hold another swinish mirror to the back of your head, force you to admit to yourself that the bald patch lying there has spread yet again territorially and is freehold.

Why do hairdressers insist on having so many voyeuring mirrors around? Have they, as a breed, like actors, a mirror fetish?

Apart from insulting you with the uncompromising reality of mirrors they also insist upon making complacent conversation.

'Have you had your holiday yet?

'Not yet.'

Snip snip snip. You know the hairdresser is desperately trying to think of something else to say. So being a nice guy, you help out.

'Have you had *your* holiday yet?'

'Not yet.'

Snip snip snip. You think: Shall I ask her where she's thinking of going when she goes? You desist. You've done your bit.

Snip snip snip. 'Do you work around here?' she asks, inspired.

You have to pay for such fascinating conversations. That big bill could not be just for the haircut. For gone are the days, alas, when a haircut cost half a crown. Now, women often cut men's hair and they do it well, very well. But a high price has to be paid to hire a Delilah.

Certainly an absurdly high price around these parts. Yesterday I went into a hairdressing Unisex emporium in Golders Green Road. It looked fairly classy with potted plants and Radio 2 wallpaper – music. The Delilahs all had clean fingernails. 'How much,' I asked, 'for a trim?' When they told me the price I had to emphasise I wanted a haircut not an operation.

I do not know why, just before I sat down at this desk, Paddy Muir came to mind. I have little in common with him. I have not seen him these many years, not since he and his wife emigrated to Canada. Yet suddenly, for no apparent reason, a minute or so before the telephone sounded, I thought of him. I walked into the hall, picked up the receiver and heard his voice. I felt curiously cold at the back of my neck. It's time, I thought, time to consult oracles, pay attention to inklings and omens. Simply, though, he was in London, and he decided well, why not, he would just telephone me, old mate, to see how I was getting on. Still writing poems are you? 'I've just had a haircut,' I said.

Coincidences. They occur all the time, increasingly, I fancy, as the years pass by, as the pages are blown over. Things happen that we knew would happen before the door opened. The feeling of having been here before. And 'déjà vu' we say, as if the mystery

58

named is the mystery solved. And 'synchronicity' we say, as if that word itself were a diagnosis and an explanation of all coincidences.

Was it Jung who first used the word 'synchronicity' to indicate a meaningful coincidence? But what was meaningful about P. Muir telephoning me 35½ minutes ago? And why am I thinking now of another coincidence, one more odd, which concerns a Saturday morning journey across London in 1948 when I was a medical student?

That morning in June, I had set out from my digs in 38 Aberdare Gardens, NW6, carrying a bag and a cricket bat, for Finchley Road underground station. I was on my way to play cricket for Westminster Hospital whose sports ground was located in those of a mental institution in South London. So I had to travel to Charing Cross, change to the Northern Line, continue to South Clapham before taking a final short bus ride.

When I entered the train at Finchley Road I was not thinking of my journey or of cricket but of a telephone conversation I had had the previous day with Louis MacNeice whom, at that time I had not met. I sat down and, soon after, overheard an animated conversation going on about poetry-drama. I looked up in surprise and with some alarm for one of the two men in conversation opposite me looked like Louis MacNeice – or rather, looked like a photograph I had seen of Louis MacNeice in a book.

At Charing Cross Station the man resembling Louis MacNeice got up and quit the carriage at the same time as I did, and on the platform I dared to stammer, 'Excuse me, are you Louis MacNeice?'

'No,' the man said, unsmilingly.

Embarrassed, I moved away as fast as I could and, in adolescent confusion, lost my way. Eventually I discovered the correct platform for trains on the Northern Line travelling south. As I approached, the doors of a waiting train began to close and I spurted forward, managing to extend my cricket bat just in time to prevent the doors shutting completely. All the doors of the train had to open again so, victoriously, if somewhat self-conscious, I strutted into the carriage.

He was sitting opposite me. He was staring at me and at my cricket bat with transparent distaste. I did not look again at Louis MacNeice's doppelganger but gazed at the back of my hand entranced almost all the way to South Clapham where, to my horror, he stood up preparing to exit.

I allowed him to get ahead of me. He shot forward purposefully; I loitered. He walked up the ascending escalator; I rested on its rail with chronic inertia. I pretended not to notice how, when he reached the top, he looked over his shoulder rather wildly.

It must have been all of three minutes before I found him at the bus queue. I had almost decided to walk but the damned bus came trundling in. Because he went downstairs I took my bat and bag upstairs.

Five minutes later when I descended, he was ready to alight also. It was incredible. We had journeyed from Finchley Road Tube Station to this same bus-stop in South Clapham. On the pavement, as the bus moved away, he swivelled towards me, pulled out his wallet, extracted delicately from it a visiting card which he offered me as proof that he was not Louis MacNeice.

'I'm not following you,' I protested vehemently. 'I'm going to play cricket in there.'

I pointed my cricket bat towards the main gates of the hospital. He followed the direction of my bat and read the big sign which indicated that these were the gates of a Mental Asylum.

Mouth open, he walked away with undignified haste.

In those post-war days when I lodged in 38 Aberdare Gardens, I often visited the cafés of Swiss Cottage. Sometimes I encountered there that gifted sculptor, William Turnbull. Last night, while watching the News on television I thought of Bill Turnbull and of a story he once told me.

On the TV screen they showed, as usual, how in Britain now, Violence no longer snores in the armchair but roams the streets. War in Northern Ireland, then war on the mainland – this time police rioting near a colliery. It is no use talking about the law, I thought, justice has its eternal statutes. Then, abruptly, the script was no longer devised by our Prime Minister for the cameras took us to Australia, to a helicopter flying over bolting wild horses. Gunners in this same helicopter were shooting them. Not all these horses died instantly. They were being slaughtered, apparently, because they had infected with TB some of the valuable cattle of the Australian plains.

But what you may ask has this to do with William Turnbull, sculptor? Bill had been in the RAF and one day, while out on exercise, his plane, along with others, flew low over the sea. When the squadron suddenly observed on shore a colony of seals, one of the planes banked down and started shooting them up. Other pilots, daft in their own adrenaline, dived down and soon all the guns were mindlessly firing *tak tak tak*, just for the hell of it. They fired and fired, the aircrews shouting loud, the guns all blazing. The seals tried to slide into the sea, the rocks and shingle a wriggling, black mass of seals. Then Bill saw it, they all saw it: the foam at the edge of the sea the colour of raw meat, a most disconcerting, shocking red.

Last night, after I turned off the News, as I sat opposite the blank television screen I wondered if Bill Turnbull had seen the shooting from the air of those frightened wild horses. If he did so, I know what he would be remembering and what colour he would be thinking of.

September 1984

At the back of letters I send off to correspondents in the USA I set down, according to custom, my address. After writing down the number of my house, the name of my street, and then London NW11 8NH, please sir, do I write England or United Kingdom or Great Britain?

England suffices, I suppose, when I write from London. Often, though, I am in Wales and send off letters from Wales. Despite the success of English imperialism, I cannot write Wales, England, for the phantom of Owain Glyndwr would breathe coldly forever down the back of my neck and share my bed. Nor can I write Wales, near England, for that description, however accurate, seems absurd. Yet I have to add some geographical location for the sake of the American mailmen who think Wales merely to be the name of the cemetery where Elizabeth Taylor wants to be buried – when she's dead, that is.

I feel ill at ease setting down United Kingdom – not because of some feminists who would name it United Queendom – but because these days we are so many nations and so disunited. We are living in a state of latent civil war not only in Northern Ireland but on the mainland also. Besides, Americans call us Brits. That suggests perhaps I should write Great Britain.

However when I have added *great* to Britain I hear distant drums roll and bugles toot. I feel grandiose claiming I am a Great Brit. Sticking on the stamp in Golders Green Post Office in Finchley Road I would feel obliged to hum to myself, 'Rule Britannia, Britannia Rules the Waves'. I can imagine how, for some reason, people would then move away from me. On the other hand, I probably would get served pronto by the usually yawning Post-Office clerk.

Great Britain? Who first used that appellation? Presumably it was a self-description but I have always understood that we, as a nation, are prone to understatement. Still, Mrs Thatcher talks about making Britain 'Great' again. To which I can only add the Welsh exclamation, 'Ach y fee'. For the very word 'great' in this context brings to my mind, and perhaps to others of my generation, those lunatics, Hitler and Mussolini, who wanted their postal addresses to be A. Hitler, Great Germany, and B. Mussolini, Great Italy.

There are occasions, of course, when boasting and immodesty are expected. Read the notices of Estate Agents. Their hyperbole matches that of Hollywood. Or look at the blurb of any book. You will find the blurb-writer using the word 'great' unblushingly.

I have just received from Robson Books an advance copy of my autobiography, *A Poet in the Family*, which is now coming out as a paperback ten years after its original publication. On the cover is a photograph of myself and beneath it the inevitable boasting quote. In this case, 'A magnificently conceived work on the author's life' – *Guardian*. (Which it is, Fred, which it verily is!)

However, I have a secret to disclose. When the publisher sent to me for my approval the rough of the cover, the quote beneath my photograph was somewhat briefer. It read, 'Magnificently conceived.' My parents, had they been alive, might have wanly smiled at that, or at least raised their eyebrows. But there is a point, as I suggested to Robson Books, where boasting goes too far.

The neighbourhood watch schemes, instigated and encouraged by the police to combat crime, are spreading. They have reached my area. I have been circularised and told the names of the ten wardens who live within a stone's throw of my house. Good luck to them. I understand that through these neighbourhood schemes the crime rate has been drastically reduced. It would be more universally reduced if the Government tackled the unemployment problem with greater commitment.

Nobody likes burglars. Not even other burglars. I have never been able to forget a cartoon I once saw in the *New Yorker* a decade or so ago. It was of a very scared, masked burglar trying to rouse a sleeping couple. The caption read: 'Wake up, wake up. There's a noise downstairs and it's not me!'

Before the American elections are over we may hear more about one Jerry Falwell, whose TV programme 'Old Time Gospel Hour' is so popular in the USA. He tells viewers that nuclear war and apocalypse are at hand. Devout Christians, however, need not worry. They have a wonderful future. 'We don't need to go to bed at night wondering if someone's going to push the button and destroy the planet between now and sunrise,' he declaims. The reason for such complacency, apparently, is that before the holocaust genuine Christians will be taken protectively straight up to Heaven by God, the Father.

It is reported that Jerry Falwell has the ear of Ronald Reagan. Certainly he is urging his mesmerised followers to vote Republican. Perhaps doubting viewers will see the menace and irony in this? Joke: We shall bomb Soviet Russia in five minutes.

Last Sunday, I thought of Jerry Falwell when I visited a nursing home in Kent. As I quit my parked car I saw a group of people, some in shade, some in sunlight. They looked weary and sick. Suddenly one of the denizens was at my side. She was one who had recently 'seen the light'. Now she said to me gently, 'The day of our death is the most beautiful day of our lives.'

I did not say to her that with such a belief she should vote

Republican. I did not respond in any way. She had, it would seem, inner peace and serenity whereas I live in this confusing world of 'I don't know'. The woman was smiling at me as I walked on. I know that smile. I have seen it depicted in a painting on the countenance of a bloodily-arrowed St Sebastian.

It is hopeless to argue with those who know the rapture of certainty, as new converts do, be they religious converts, born-again communists, or whatever. For converts find intelligible our unintelligible world, hear sweet dialectical harmony where we listen to dissonance, see a clear pattern where we observe only amorphous mass. And should we present them with contradictory facts how soon these are adapted, fitted, interfused into the harmony or pattern.

All this makes me recall a patient who came into the Casualty Department declaring he was dead. He was certain of this. It was his unshakable belief. When asked if dead men can bleed he replied, 'Of course not.' One of the doctors, then, with a pin drew a little blood on the back of his forearm. The patient stared at it, startled. 'That just goes to show,' he said, 'that dead men do bleed, doctor.'

Research scientists imbued with a relentless spirit of enquiry are a rum lot, admirable though many of them may be. Think of those doctors such as John Hunter who audaciously experimented on themselves for the sake of suffering humankind.

Many watching the TV over-dramatised biography of Sigmund Freud will be reminded of his over-enthusiastic use of cocaine. What a bloodier meal the BBC drama department could have made of another cocaine story: that of the German surgeon August Bier and his assistant Hildenbrandt who, together, initiated the practice of spinal anaesthesia.

It was in the summer of 1898 that Bier suggested to his assistant that they inject cocaine into the spinal fluid before an operation rather than administer a general anaesthetic. First, though, they needed to discover whether this procedure would be effective, would delete the pain of major surgery. It was no use experimenting on animals. The creatures could not give the necessary subjective evidence, could not talk. So they injected cocaine into their own cerebro-spinal fluids before recording their sensations to pain-stimuli with teutonic thoroughness.

For instance, the injection having been given to Hildenbrandt, Bier made an incision in the skin of his assistant's leg, making blood flow. Hildenbrandt blithely remarked that he merely felt the mild pressure of the scalpel. Minutes later Bier grasped a long thick needle and plunged it through the muscles of Hildebrandt's thigh until it grated against the bone. 'I'm feeling nothing,' Hildenbrandt exclaimed delightedly.

Bier lit a cigar and I can imagine how, momentarily, the two men stared at each other before Bier brought down his lit cigar to the skin. His assistant smelt his own flesh burning out but experienced no pain. August Bier picked up a heavy hammer. 'Go ahead,' said Hildenbrandt – in German, of course.

We have our own intrepid scientists in Britain, now, experimenting on themselves. One such is Professor Brindley who works in the Department of Physiology at the Institute of Psychiatry in South East London. With colleagues he has been conducting experiments that could lead to an organic treatment of impotence. He has reported in the *Lancet* that he has injected substances that caused erections lasting two to five hours. Some patients suffered them longer – sorry about that pun – up to forty hours. Such priapism of course is no joking matter. It is a condition terribly distressful as Professor Brindley could testify, for on experimenting on himself, as well as on other volunteers, he, too, suffered a sustained priapism.

Priapism outside the laboratory is far from common but it can be a most painful side-effect of certain modern drugs. So great credit to the professor because he has now probably discovered an effective therapy for it. For after taking the drug metaraminol he was able to report, 'The smallest dose (0.4 mg) caused conspicuous shrinkage of the penis lasting one and a half hours. During this time it was difficult but not impossible to obtain a psychogenic or reflex erection.'

I shake my head in astonishment. I know that one should be solemn about advances in the treatment of impotence or priapism but I cannot help but smile to myself as I picture the professor sitting in his laboratory, ruler in one hand, stop watch in the other, looking down and excitedly shouting, 'Eureka! Eureka!'

*

We took our holiday late this year – in the South of France. We had not visited France for more than a decade and my schoolboy French has deteriorated further. I had to leave all conversations to my wife. After all, one must shut up irrevocably if on asking for bread at a restaurant one is served with a rabbit.

So I sat on the beach, silent as a monk, reading Peter Ackroyd's biography of T. S. Eliot which had been sent to me for review, thinking how despite that poet's worldly success his life-story was threaded with chapters of ill-health and unhappiness. Or I reclined staring at the sea, thinking of nothing, or remembering my own past (nostalgie de l'enfance), or wondering about the invisible colour that rests between the last and first of the rainbow. Or I simply looked about me at the topless ones with pleasure and occasional priapism.

Of course, making conversation in English, in England, can be difficult – real conversation I mean, the kind of creative conversation where 'one can fccl at home'. How can one talk, for instance, to those who have specialized so much that they have little interest outside their specialty – e.g., nuclear physics? We are living in an age of incrcasing specialization, technology and cultural barbarism. No wonder most conversations are clichéd and tedious.

I am not suggesting that my own interests and knowledge are wide. I am ignorant of so many things. Dance, for instance. I am simply not interested in the ballet. Once, at a Foyle's Literary Lunch I was placed next to Dame Ninette de Valois. I tried hard to think of something to say to that beautiful old lady. The soup bowl was empty and still we had not exchanged more than a smile and a 'how-do-you-do'. Desperate, I blurted out, 'I'm afraid I know nothing about Dance.' Then I stupidly added, 'But I am interested in Football.'

Dame Ninette de Valois stared at her soup plate, obviously troubled. At last the soup plates were whisked away and she turned to me and said triumphantly, 'I know little of Poetry. But I danced for Yeats. You see, he chanted his poems and I danced to them.'

Ninette de Valois. Would that, I wonder, be a French name?

Of all reported conversations the one between William Blake and the portrait painter, Thomas Phillips, amuses me most. Their talk touched on angels. Now Blake believed, without doubt, that angels descended literally for the great painters and sat for their portraits.

'We hear much,' said Phillips, 'of the grandeur of Michelangelo; from the engravings I should say he's been over-rated; he could not paint an angel as well as Raphael.'

'He's not over-rated, Sir,' replied Blake. 'And he could paint an angel better than Raphael.'

'But you've never seen paintings of Michelangelo. Perhaps your friends' opinions have deceived you.'

'I speak from the opinion of a friend who could not be mistaken,' Blake stated. 'I mean the Archangel Gabriel . . . I was reading Young's *Night Thoughts* and I came to the passage "Who can paint an Angel?" And a voice answered "Michelangelo. I know I sat for him. I am the Archangel Gabriel." '

Blake went on to explain that he knew it truly was the Archangel when he looked from whence the voice came and saw a shining shape with bright wings much diffused in light. Blake continued, 'As I looked the shape dilated more and more: he waved his hands, the roof of my study opened; he ascended into heaven.'

Thomas Phillips marvelled at this wild story. And so he should have done. It would be a hell of a thing, would it not, to find Blake sitting next to one at a Foyle's Literary Lunch?

Nostalgie de l'enfance. I heard someone in the street whistling 'Danny Boy'. At once I recalled from the gone years my mother's voice singing to me the words of that melancholy song.

> The summer's gone and the last rose is falling
> Tis you, tis you, must go and I must bide.

An appropriate song for this moody time of the year. The white rose is withering. So many white things have fallen away: the white blossom of spring; the white flowers, the white paired butterflies of summer. Gone this 1984. Shall there be some more white things, snow perhaps, later?

Already, while walking the streets of Hampstead these fading evenings, after the balmy airs of Southern France, I turn my collar up, I see my breath smoke in the air. In the distance, I fancy that I can observe The Ghost of Winter walking this way. Under the furthest lamp-post look how he turns towards us to reveal his utterly pale face.

October 1984

I want to record two recent encounters, one with Eddie whom no doubt I shall soon forget, the other with Emile whom I shall remember always.

In a Hampstead pub I was asked by one of the bar-lolling denizens ('I'm Eddie,' he said') about the dangers of the asbestos fall-out from the great fire at Cricklewood. Six weeks ago, it was reported that one and a half tons of asbestos debris fountained up into the air and was gently scattered over clandestine places in the borough of Brent. My new-found friend of quarter of an hour was not sanguine. 'The prevailing winds,' he said, 'come from the South West towards Hampstead. That flaming fire was less than a mile away as the black crow flies.'

Further conversation with Eddie revealed that he was not only a gloomy fellow who knew there were no frontiers for flying asbestos between Brent and Camden but one who also had no faith in his own body physiology. Of course, that is true of all hypochondriacs: they do not trust their own bodies. They know their health depends precariously on the amazing balancing machinery of billions and billions and billions of complicated body cells. Sod's Law declares to them that something is sure to go wrong if not on Monday, then on Tuesday, especially if there are fires in Cricklewood.

I do not mock hypochondriacs however often they put out their tongues at the mirror or stare with peculiar sadness at their own faeces in the lavatory bowl. I was once a medical student and all medical students become temporary hypochondriacs. When I first walked the wards at Westminster Hospital and observed a patient recovering from a coronary I secretly took my own pulse. When I gazed at the chest X-ray on the illuminated, oblong screen and saw there the mischievous shadow of a neoplasm, back in my own room, later, I listened with my new stethoscope to my own chest. When the consultant neurologist, Dr Meadows, examined a lady with multiple sclerosis and declared how, twenty years earlier, she had experienced a transient blindness, I began to feel my own eyes go out of focus. And soon after leaving the operating theatre, having watched for the first time an appendix being removed, I suddenly suffered an inordinate amount of painful wind in my right iliac fossa. Perhaps the only time I felt entirely healthy was when I was doing my midwifery!

So I shall not mock hypochondriacs. I shall not mock Hampstead Eddie. I shall not mock myself. I live even nearer to the Cricklewood Conflagration than he does and asbestos fallout is a serious matter. For there is no known safe exposure limit to the blue or brown variety. Doctors are aware, though, that there is a powerful synergistic effect between these asbestos fibres and tobacco smoke.

'So if those exposed to such asbestos give up smoking, Eddie,' I said, 'after eighteen months their statistical chances of suffering a lung cancer would be reduced by more than ten times.'

'They should have signs – "No Smoking in Hampstead",' the barmaid said who had overheard our conversation.

Eddie dragged at his cigarette with anxious vehemence and then began to cough. When I left the pub I could not help but notice which way the wind was blowing.

I had arranged to visit a College of Education at Stoke-on-Trent in the afternoon and then drive a further ninety miles to the University town where I was scheduled to give a poetry reading in the evening. I was beginning to feel sorry that I had agreed to undertake such an arduous jaunt especially when a Dr Margaret Smith of the English Department at the University telephoned me and asked me to be there at 6 p.m. I could not be there that early.

'We'd like to give you dinner first,' she said. 'The reading will be at 8 p.m.'

Reluctantly I agreed to meet her at the forecourt of the local railway station at the compromise time of 6.45 p.m. Leaving Stoke I already felt somewhat tired as a result of the morning drive up the growling M1 and M6 from Golders Green and from the holding forth in the afternoon classroom. And now I had to drive much too fast into the sunset to keep my appointment with Dr Smith.

Amazingly, though, I arrived at the station at 6.45 p.m. exactly. A short young woman (Dr Smith) and a tall younger man (a student called Emile) strolled lazily towards me as I climbed stiffly out of my car. They did not know how many lorry drivers I had cursed, how I had taken various bends on two wheels. I stood there slightly shaking, proud of my punctuality, but as exhausted as a stunt man's understudy. I needed a wash and a rest. It was years since I had left Golders Green.

Dr Smith insisted, 'First come to the restaurant and eat, then we'll take you to The Garth Hotel which is near the University.' I allowed her to persuade me. The table was waiting. I did not know the waiter was not waiting. He had the soul of a snail and took hours to reach our table. At 7.30 p.m. I had spooned one avocado pear and sipped a glass of white wine. 'I do need to go to the hotel and sort myself out before the reading,' I sighed.

So Emile was commanded to take me to The Garth Hotel (so near the University where the reading was to take place) while Dr Smith paid the bill. She would meet me in ten minutes time. Emile would jump into my car and direct me to the hotel pronto.

Alas, Emile lost his way. We turned right, we turned left, we turned left again, and soon, at 8 p.m. we had returned from whence we had started. At that moment my audience at the University were, no doubt, settling themselves.

'Christ, Emile,' I said, 'I've travelled a helluva way and fast to get here on time.'

Emile, a born pedestrian if ever there was one, blamed the one way system. He stated that he knew the wrong turning taken, so we set off again. Once more he lost his way. At 8.10 p.m. he cried out triumphantly, 'It's just around the corner. I know where I am.' I drove the car speedily around the corner where he shouted, 'There it is.' It looked more like a dismal, sow-coloured pub than an hotel to me. It was a dismal, sow-coloured pub. I parked the car aghast, thinking, 'God, they could have found me a better place to stay than this.'

But there was no time to lose. We pushed the doors open into the noise of a jukebox. Above its harsh soundings Emile declared masterfully to the man behind the bar busily engaged serving a couple, 'This is Dr Dannie Abse. There's a room here booked for him.' The barman gestured to the stairs that started from a distant alcove. I ran towards these carrying my bag, leaving Emile standing. I ran up the stairs to a corridor, to a door, opened it. Surprise, surprise, here was peace, a spacious bedroom, a sleepy-looking, tidy double bed. I looked at my watch. 8.15. They would have to wait, I decided.

I tested the bed, pulled back the eiderdown and sheets. I needed a wash, I needed a pee. No washbasin, though over a Windsor chair I espied a towel. I took the towel and investigated the corridor that owned yet another door which I opened. There was, as the estate agents say, a well-appointed bathroom, scented soap, every convenience.

Back in my room I changed my sticky shirt, put my pyjamas under the pillow, threw the towel accurately towards the chair, pulled out the books I needed to read from, then in laundered glory, descended the stairs into the shadowy alcove where Emile loitered anxiously, biting his nails. 'It's gone quarter past,' he accused me.

'Don't get lost this time,' I responded, knowing the University was near at hand.

In the car once more we turned right, turned left, screeched around several corners. Emile, unbelievably, had lost his way yet again. As we hesitated at one crossroads, wondering whether to go left or right I noticed opposite me a sign on a building which read The Garth Hotel.

'Emile,' I asked, in what a cliché-loving writer would describe as a strangled voice, 'Emile, didn't Dr Smith say that my hotel was The Garth?'

'Yes,' said Emile.

'Where the hell did you take me?'

'I must have made a mistake. But there's no time for you to register now. We must get to the University.'

'Emile, you schlemiel,' I said, 'I've got to go back and get my case, my pyjamas, my toothbrush, shaving stuff, Christ.'

I thought how I must have gone into somebody's private bedroom, somebody's private bathroom, tested somebody's private bed, used somebody's private towel, etc., etc. Probably the room was the publican's own pride and joy. If I didn't go back to that sow-coloured pub now I would never be able to find the place again. We arrived back there this time fortunately without mishap. Emile waited in the car, somewhat white-faced. I ran into the pub. I did not look at the barman. I zipped into the alcove and up the stairs. I ran down the corridor and into the bedroom. Thank heavens nobody was occupying it. I collected my pyjamas and my bag and returned down the stairs, sprinted to the door and into the car. We arrived at the University and at the next stroke it was 8.40 p.m. precisely.

There is something wrong with me. These days I hardly ever dream Walter Mitty daydreams. No longer, as the number 13 bus trundles through autumn and Swiss Cottage do I bring down my conker against my opponent's to become the Conker King. Between two bus stops, approaching Lord's, as I sit upstairs, I no longer replay the old remarkable game of cricket when, with a broken arm, I hit a six to make Glamorgan the champion County. How many elegiac years have passed since that same bus magically transformed itself into a nightclub, smokily lit, bare-armed, while I played the piano and sang, better than Fats Waller, 'Aint Misbehavin' while the audience listened enraptured until some fool shouted in my left ear, as if I were deaf, 'Any fares please?'

It hardly happens any more. It did last week, though, after a telephone call inviting me to be an auctioneer, along with David Benedictus, Humphrey Burton and Melvyn Bragg, in aid of Amnesty International. 'An auction of prints by Auerbach, Kitaj, Elisabeth Frink, Josef Herman, Joe Tilson, Milein Cosman and many others,' I was told. 'At noon, Saturday, October 27th at the Friends' Meeting House in Hampstead.' But I had to be elsewhere on that date.

After I put the phone down I slipped, in the old way, into reverie. In no time at all there I was, a hero, high up there on the rostrum, hoarse and shouting (oddly), 'How much for her beautiful head, how much for her beautiful legs, how much for her red-buried heart? C'mon bid, bid, bid. I'll give you a hammer of ebony, nails of silver, too, and a varnished plank of pine to hit the nails right through. So bid, bid, bid and going, going, gone, says the little pink worm.'

'What's the matter with you?' asked my wife.

'I, er,' I said.

Amnesty International. I stopped daydreaming and thought instead of the reality of why such an organization exists. It is hard, if one lives in comfortable liberty, to think for long of all the damp, dark, dangerous dungeons of the world wherein lie so many political prisoners. I recently had a visit from a Polish friend who told me of the plight of a poet I know who had supported Solidarity like so many others. He is not in a cell and yet he is not truly at liberty either. A man not allowed to work whether in a colliery or at a desk is not fully at liberty. There are many ways of condemning a man.

So many important European poets have been subjected to grim social pressures which we writers in Britain have largely escaped. Lorca was murdered, Mayakovsky committed suicide, Mandelstam disappeared, Hernandez died in a Franco prison, Celan survived a Nazi concentration camp, Brecht was exiled, Pasternak in disgrace. Of course, some poets survived and later made unforgettable direct or indirect artefacts of their experience. The best poet now writing in Poland, Zbigniew Herbert, has written, 'I think that the war created all the problems of my writing: what a man is in the face of death, how he behaves in the presence of a totalitarian threat. . . .'

Mandelstam's wife spoke of one way to react when threatened. 'I often wondered,' she wrote, 'whether it is right to scream when you are being beaten and trampled underfoot. Isn't it better to face one's tormentors in a stance of satanic pride, answering them with contemptuous silence? I decided that it is better to scream. This pitiful sound, which sometimes, goodness knows how, reaches into the remotest prison cell, is a concentrated expression of the last vestige of human dignity. It is a man's way of leaving a trace, of telling people how he lived and died. By his screams he asserts his right to live, sends a message to the outside world demanding help and calling for resistance. If nothing is left one must scream. Silence is the real crime against humanity.'

What the coercive authorities prefer most, of course, is silence. But screaming messages do come through rather like that of Dan Pagis who survived annihilation by Hitler and who later composed this brief poem called 'Written in Pencil in the Sealed Railway-Car':

> here in the carload
> i am eve
> with abel my son
> if you see my other son
> cain son of man
> tell him i

There are many silences and not all are of the grave. 'Silence everybody,' says the worst and last Auctioneer. Totalitarian societies, meanwhile, take a lease on that irrevocable silence and would not have those articulate ever forget it. Another Polish poet, Tymoteusz Karpowicz, has said it better than I can in this 'Lesson of Silence':

> Whenever a butterfly
> happened to fold
> too violently its wings –
> there was a call: silence, please!
>
> As soon as one feather
> of a startled bird
> jostled against a ray –
> there was a call: silence, please!
>
> In that way we were taught
> how to walk without noise
> the elephant on his drum,
> man on his earth.
>
> The trees were rising
> mute above the fields
> as rises the hair
> of the horror-stricken.

The orthodox Medical Establishment is very careful these days when expressing its opinion about the value of Alternative Medicine – homeopathy, acupuncture etc., because of the Royal Family's sympathy towards such therapy. Prince Charles has sounded off, 'What is taken for today's unorthodoxy is probably going to be tomorrow's convention.'

This is a most dubious judgement. Most unorthodox remedies simply disappear from view – they remind one of traditional prescriptions such as are recommended in present day Nigeria: Remedy for guinea worms – if the guinea worm in your body comes out like a thread, bake it and put one tooth of a dead person on it. Then bind the two together with a white piece of cloth. Use this to rub your body over, nine times. Then go and bury it. You will never be attacked by guinea worms again.

My own brushes with way-out medicasters, even those who have a medical qualification, have left me more sceptical than ever. Take acupuncture. I happened to visit an old doctor who had come out of retirement to practise it. As we chatted about one of his patients, a well-known actress, he suddenly said, 'I'll give it to you. That'll convince you. You're not relaxed. You'll see how it relaxes you.'

He suddenly shot behind my chair and pressed his thumbs deep through my jacket and shirt into the flesh above my shoulder blades. Now when pressure is exerted there it always hurts a little, so when he said, pressing like mad, 'Now, doesn't that hurt?' I had to nod assent. He stood above me triumphantly, 'I told you. You're not relaxed.'

I felt utterly relaxed. However I did not want to disappoint him, and I only hesitated momentarily when he asked me to take off my jacket and roll up my sleeves. Swiftly he stuck acupuncture needles into my arms. One thing I learnt anyway: acupuncture is not a painful procedure.

I sat there idiotically like St Sebastian, chatting away until I felt I could say 'I really must go now.' After he took the needles out of my arms I rolled down my sleeves. Meanwhile he was behind the chair again pressing my shoulders, this time very gently, with his thumbs. 'Does that hurt?' he asked. 'No,' I replied. He was greatly pleased.

The old doctor was not deliberately fraudulent. I think he was fooling himself – unaware that the first time he thumbed me he did so with frenetic passion unlike his second tender attempt.

'But what about acupuncture in China today?' I hear him and the Prince of Wales argue. 'Do they not operate on people there who simply have had acupuncture instead of a general anaesthetic? That surely demonstrates the power of acupuncture over pain.'

Chinese official documents of 1972 stated that acupuncture anaesthesia was 'usually performed by a young girl of 20–25 who is politically sincere and who spends 2–3 days in advance of the operation encouraging the patient in his mental attitude, especially towards the works and thoughts of Chairman Mao.'

As Petr Skrabanek has commented in the *Lancet* 'The mystery of acupuncture anaesthesia largely evaporates when we learn that it was supplemented by a premedication, local anaesthesia with procaine, an intravenous drip with pethidine and other drugs.' Even then only some twelve per cent of patients were thought suitable for acupuncture anaesthesia. Worse, a number of them still felt the pain of the operation.

Maybe I've got it all wrong. Certainly next time I allow myself to be acupunctured I'll spend 2–3 days first getting my attitude right by considering the medical thoughts of our Prince of Wales.

November 1984

Every other Thursday morning I sit down at my desk to write the next instalment of my 1984 Diary. After cleaning my teeth, after picking up the letters from the hall-mat, after eating my buttered toast, drinking my two cups of tea (milk with one sugar, since I know you are all agog to know), after indulging in other enormously commonplace activities that any Cabinet Minister would immediately transcribe into his diaries for posterity, I reach my desk and the blank page on which I will write Abse's 1984.

At this moment, since unvarnished truth in diaries must be told, my mind is full of other writers' journals. For before going to bed last night (I sleep on the right-hand side of a double bed) I watched on TV an admirably produced, adapted and well-acted film feature of Boswell's *London Diary*, unboundedly open in its communication; and not ten minutes ago while reading *The Times* over breakfast (and mumbling yet again, Why don't we take the *Guardian?*) I alighted on a book review of *The Castle Diaries* by Woodrow Wyatt of bow-tie fame.

Apparently, these diaries, even abridged, contain a half a million words. Wyatt suggests that should a research student in some distant future pick his way through the unabridged version lodged in one or another University Library, then that student should promptly be certified as insane. In kinder mood, Woodrow Wyatt adds that 'there are some nuggets to be extracted' and with blithe pincers he pulls them out one by one for our delectation. Barbara Castle's hatred of Callaghan – 'Frankly I believe Jim Callaghan is capable of anything'; Harold Wilson's drinking habits – 'I think he had been taking comfort in his brandy again'; Roy Jenkins's ataraxic presence – 'My private tête-à-tête with Roy took place one lunch at No 11. Why do I feel constrained at these intimate talks?' Nuggets, every one of them, Mr Wyatt assures us.

Perhaps they are. I remember the *Crossman Diaries, Volume III*. Wonderful nuggets there: 'I had a horrible office lunch of particularly disgusting sandwiches'; '. . . at 2 a.m. my stomach evacuated totally. . .'; 'I lunched at the Ritz with Peregrine Worsthorne'; and pure gold this – 'before Cabinet I had a frantic message that Tony Crosland wanted to lunch with me. I took him to lunch. (I don't know why he doesn't take me, perhaps because he doesn't have a club.) So off we went to the Athenaeum where I gave him grouse and claret.'

Politicians such as Crossman and Castle believe that their red-hot diary insertions will one day be of historical value. 'Back to a late reception at Lancaster House for the Commonwealth Prime Ministers' Conference. George Brown was rolling round (sic) distressingly sozzled.' (Castle); 'I went off to put up plaques at a couple of health centres and then I drove to Coventry to address the annual dinner of The College of Midwives with Doris Butterworth, Jolly Jack's wife, who is their President, in the chair.' (Crossman).

Why do so many people, other than politicians, keep diaries? I suspect that the majority of them are unsure of their identities and perhaps feel themselves, too often, to be half-dead like convicts in a prison. Diary-keeping, then, can be a therapeutic exercise, a prescription to prove to themselves that they are alive. Like the imperative diary pages of a prisoner their words proclaim, 'I am here, I am alive, I thought this, I did that.'

So meaningful can diary-keeping be that its author's life may be changed by it. It can become a dangerous activity. Even Boswell realized that he might have sought out certain adventures in order that he could claim them for his diary. Those who succumb to such temptations are rather like those tourists with busy cameras who only visit Venice, say, in order to return with snapshots of themselves standing amongst the pigeons of St Mark's Square or in front of the Doge's Palace. They may not have enjoyed the pleasurable offerings of Venice but, by damn, they have wonderful souvenirs in their albums.

Diary-keeping, though, can work as a moral force. It has been asserted that by the act of confessing their sins Catholics are not only allowed consolation but the very prospect of confession is an effective prophylactic. It is embarrassing for them to whisper to the priest yet again that, on Monday, they coveted their neighbour's wife, on Tuesday they masturbated, and that, on Wednesday, they committed adultery. In the same way the diarist may not wish to confess to his diary one more act of meanness and of spite and so behaves himself instead. Velleities do not become desires and desires do not become overt acts because of the power of the word on a page.

It is not comfortable, though, to be with one who obsessionally keeps a diary. Lately I was in Lancashire with the Welsh poet, Gillian Clarke. I was telling her about a cartoon I had seen concerning Reagan and Mondale. The cartoon showed Reagan with his Cabinet – Reagan was asleep. It also showed Mondale with his Cabinet – the Cabinet were asleep. 'It was that Republican Bob Hope who remarked that Mondale had had a charisma by-pass operation,' I added. Gillian laughed and said, 'I'll put that in my diary.' When I told her later about an incident involving a common friend of ours she said, 'Oh yes, I'll definitely put that in my diary tonight.' Because Gillian seemed to keep her midnight diary with such implacable regularity I began to feel bugged. I found myself thereafter being cautious about what I said, what I did.

Some writers, of course, bug themselves. The Goncourt brothers recorded how Victor Hugo 'always has a note book in his pocket and if, in conversation with you, he happens to express the tiniest thought, to put forward the smallest idea, he promptly turns away from you, takes out his note book and writes down what he has just said.' Thanks to the Goncourts, practised buggers, Hugo, the self-bugger, was bugged.

If I kept a diary with the conscientious ardour of Gillian Clarke or Virginia Woolf, say, who kept diaries between 1915–1941, thirty volumes of them, I think I would feel guilty. In a diary a writer is talking to himself, in other forms of prose, even autobiography, the writer is speaking to others. And it is a writer's job, is it not, to address others, however few these may seem to be? Virginia Woolf felt guilty when she devoted herself to her diary rather as I would if, instead of working, I slouched off in scowling truancy, on rainy weekday afternoons, to the Odeon. Virginia Woolf scolded herself for 'the lawless exercise' of writing diaries, for not addressing herself to the much more difficult task of shaping a novel.

Yet, of course, most diaries presuppose another reader. For instance, when André Gide confesses in his journals to using a chamber pot one night, why does he add firmly that this is not his usual habit? Gide knows perfectly well what his nocturnal micturating habits are, so whom is he addressing? I believe firmly that the diarist is one who likes to have secrets but he hopes that one day, maybe tomorrow, maybe centuries hence, those secrets will be whispered to others – the more the better.

Moreover, when his diaries are finally published – I was here, I was a great fellow – he is not so open to the wrath of critics as novelists, poets, and autobiographers are. Diaries pretend to be spontaneous effusions, to be defenceless, unpremeditated scribblings and as such are not only self-indulgent but beg the indulgence of reader and critic. As I do now.

Excitement. It is not every day that one receives an invitation to visit Turkey. It seemed that Cevat Capan, a celebrated Turkish writer, had translated a whole battery of 20th century British poets and that his one-man anthology is soon to be published. So the dynamic Mrs Yildiz Arda of the Turk-Ingiliz Kultur Dernegi, plus the British Council, asked me to deliver lectures at several Turkish universities on post-war British poetry and, in addition, to read from my own work at the Turco-British Associations in Istanbul and Ankara.

I expressed doubts. After all I'm not too well understood in Golders Green. Besides, my pigeon-Welsh is better than my Turkish. 'You'll find your audiences will understand English poetry better than the denizens of Golders Green,' I was told somewhat drily.

I could not imagine Turkey. Soon enough, at Heathrow, I was

boarding a magic Turkish carpet powered by a Boeing engine and three and a half hours later I alighted, blinking, in Istanbul. Already the wounded sunset shifted its coloured mobiles over the Bosphorus. I stood there, somewhat concussed, as the waters in slow knots passed under the gigantic bridge that spans Europe and Asia.

The bridge resembled, in a magnified way, the Severn Bridge – it was designed by the same engineer. 'The eighth bridge?' I suggested brilliantly, though nobody, of course, raised a diplomatic smile. 'It's their faulty English,' I consoled myself.

Next morning, before you could say Abse Pasha, my generous hosts whisked me off to view the Topkapi Palace, the oldest of the remaining palaces in the world, the Harem section of it alone containing 400 rooms, many of which faced pleasant small inner courts. It doesn't look too much like Cardiff Castle.

In the Harem building I imagined all those hand-picked, dark-eyed concubines, the Sultan yawning, lying back on cushions, spitting sherbert, while musicians plucked and blew. Wasn't this, as Yeats fancied, the country of animal sensuality? But suppose the Sultan had an Oedipus complex, or was mournfully impotent. How terrible, then, to be living there in the torture of so much available, voluptuous femininity. 'An aged man is but a paltry thing, A tattered coat upon a stick . . .'

'Stop it,' I said. Think prose, I told myself. Imagine, rather, Byzantium trees made of gold and silver with artificial birds singing, imagine the ghosts of the mosaic workers, the illuminators of sacred books, the craftsmen of jewellery, and leave the concubines alone. My hosts moved our caravans, the dogs barked and soon enough I arrived, shoeless, in the serene hush of the Blue Mosque, and later into that of St Sophia. So much enclosed space under huge semi-domes. So much to inspect closely and to relish.

In Istanbul the lectures and readings did not prompt complaints. Nobody threw knives or Turkish Delight. Afterwards, when I was taken out to dinner, we had to pass down a narrow, dimly lit alleyway. There a man stood waving the oncoming traffic of people to one side, for he was guarding two cats who were copulating under the one lamppost. I was surprised at their outrageous sensuality. I always thought cats to be secretive creatures. I have heard their oriental cries, of course, but never seen them fastened to each other. Maybe English cats, so well-bred, are more reticent than their Turkish counterparts?

We walked on and I asked Mike Winter, one of the British Council representatives in Istanbul, whether he thought that the anonymous cat-guard was simply a kind, conscientious lover of cats – or was he just a voyeur? Before he could reply one of our party known as Ginger, an American lady married to a Turk, related how only weeks earlier she had encountered another two cats copulating and a man had stood there throwing stones at these feline lovers. She had suggested that the stone thrower desist, leave the cats alone, and that nature should be allowed healthily to take its course.

'But it's not healthy, it's two male cats,' the man protested, picking up another stone.

At the first University I visited in Ankara, before I delivered my lecture, a lunch was arranged to which all the English Faculty professors, associate professors etc. were invited. I sat opposite the Dean who told me with evident satisfaction, 'We've had Elizabeth Jane Howard, Arnold Wesker and Margaret Drabble before you. If Shakespeare was alive we'd have him too.'

At Ankara I was worked hard but I did have one afternoon to visit the Hittite Museum. There I gazed at primitive implements, at messages from pre-recorded history as well as at recondite writings on ancient stone. I recalled a Hittite ritual prescription against pestilence which I had once read in one of my favourite books, *Ancient Near Eastern Texts*, edited by James B. Pritchard – a book to take to Roy Plomley's Desert Island: 'These are the words of Uhha-muwas, the Arzawaman. If people are dying in the country and if some god of the enemy is to blame then drive up one ram. Twine together blue wool, red wool, yellow wool, black wool and white wool, make it into a crown and crown the ram with it. Drive the ram on to the road leading to the enemy and while doing so speak as follows: whatever god from the enemy-land has caused this plague – see! how we drive this crowned ram to pacify thee, o god. We drive the crowned ram towards the enemy.' It's the sort of thing we normally chant at football matches, especially in Turkey after we sing 'Eight-nil, Eight-nil.'

That same night I went to a party given by Frank Taylor, the British Council representative in Ankara. There I met a dramatist recently released from prison and learnt something of the darker, more averted side of Turkey. But the Life and Soul of the party proved to be the French Cultural Attaché. He shone, he sparkled like a diamond in floodlight, he wittily discussed the national characteristics of the Turks, the Dutch, the Russians. He also dilated on the ignorance of the peasants in Eastern Turkey. Why did I want to defend them, why did I argue, I wonder? To illustrate my point I told the old joke of a Londoner who stopped his car in deepest Somerset to ask the way to Bristol. 'Is it that way?' he asked. 'Oi don't know,' replied the countryman. 'Is it the other way then?' Again the Somerset man shook his head, saying, 'Oi don't know.' 'Well, is it straight on?' 'Oi don't know.' Exasperated, our city slicker sneered, 'You don't know much, do you?' Slowly the Somerset man replied, 'That may be so. But I baint be lost.'

Flying back to Istanbul, to the generous care of Yildiz Arda, I bought the *Turkish Daily News*, the only English newspaper in Turkey. Already I knew something of its reputation, how for instance it was bravely unafraid to criticize the government's monetarist policies which had not only *not* cured inflation but had also led to a deterioration in general living standards. The *Daily News* also had a less enviable reputation for misprints. Someone, I can't remember who, had told me how after the attempted assassination of Reagan the *Daily News* reported that the President had been under the surgeon's wife for six hours.

Now, though, in the plane, I spotted very few misprints – less than you would find on an average day in the *Guardian*. I read with interest the world League Table of workers' wages per hour expressed in terms of dollars:

Norway	9.66	Japan	6.28
Belgium	9.14	France	6.07
Switzerland	8.65	Britain	5.46
USA	8.60	Spain	3.87
Canada	8.50	Hong Kong	1.65
Denmark	7.97	Taiwan	1.64
Sweden	7.91	Portugal	1.28
Australia	7.85	TURKEY	1.19
West Germany	7.54	India	0.71
Italy	6.35	China	0.26

Afterwards I turned to the inside page and was amazed to read there how a certain inhabitant of Ankara, lost in deepest Eastern Turkey, asked his way to Bitlis. 'Right? Left? Straight on?' 'Don't know.' 'You don't know much, do you?' 'No, but I'm not lost.' Somebody at the party obviously worked for the paper, and, hard up for copy, had used my joke. I had a terrific sense of triumph. I had visited Turkey and, as you see, had anonymously left my mark. Well done, me. Not many poets do that.

December 1984

I am trying to look back over the bumpy months of 1984, but I continue too fast in reverse, for I keep thinking of 1974. In May of that year I was about to quit my temporary job in the USA as Writer-In-Residence at Princeton University. Then I was asked to stay on.

I hesitated. It had been pleasurable living in Princeton – a locus not unlike Hampstead, with its duplicate of an Everyman cinema, ready at a blink to show *Blue Angel* or *The Battleship Potemkin*, with its own coffee houses such as you'd find opposite Hampstead Tube station, alleyways such as Perrins Court, similar notices in the 'High Street' pinned on to the bark of pavement trees. In addition, of course, adjacent to that 'High Street' were, as in an architect's dream, imitation Oxford Colleges.

Yes, it was pleasant there, but I missed Britain too much. How easy it was to be a patriot abroad: to take pride in a BBC that countenanced no advertisements; to boast of our other cultural institutions and of our more serious newspapers; above all, despite Northern Ireland, to state that Britain was, more or less, a caring society, believing in the ideal of full employment and somewhat concerned about its aged and its sick.

'Look at our National Health Service,' I'd say to American friends. 'Why, look at our police force even. They aren't armed as yours are. And they are respected, kept on a short leash.'

True, that 1973–4 winter, there had been the disconsolate aggro and discomfort of the three day week which I had missed. But that was over now. Britain was on the road to becoming almost itself. The USA with all its private affluence had outrageous disadvantages. Even in agreeable, middle-class Princeton, one experienced, occasionally, a taste of the other America.

For instance, in February, my young son suffered a worrying earache, presumably the result of a potent infection. So I telephoned the local Ear, Nose and Throat specialist. His secretary responded, 'He'll see your son in two weeks.'

I explained that the boy had a high temperature. 'Sorry, he's very busy,' his secretary said. I asserted that I was a British doctor, that my young son probably had an acute otitis media and would my American colleague therefore examine him urgently as I had no instrument to examine his eardrums?

The secretary went away. I listened to the silence of the telephone receiver. She returned eventually to say, 'Since you're a doctor he'll see your son next week, on Tuesday.' I fumed. I thought I must get hold of some antibiotics. I thought that if this could happen in civilized Princeton then what would happen out there in the American sticks? 'At home, with the National Health Service,' I pondered, 'sick youngsters would not be kept waiting like this.'

I declined the generous invitation to remain in the USA. Though grateful for my experience of Princeton, I returned home and was glad to be back in caring Britain. But now, in 1984, I ask myself, 'Am I at home? If so, who has come to occupy it like a vandal? Who has set class against class, North against South? Who sanctions the scandal of increasing unemployment so that the spirit of hooliganism stalks the land? Who is dismantling our National Health Service? Whose police are these, disguised in their metallic accoutrements, combating the wrath of miners and their families?'

In Yorkshire, in Durham, in Ayrshire, in South Wales, in Kent, violence is being done to whole communities. And these sleepy people have now come awake. As Duncan Bush has put it in the current issue of *Poetry Wales*, 'The villages are no longer aggregates of dwellings privatized by television but communities again, the rented videos and tapes back in the shop . . . and meetings

> in workmen's clubs and miners' welfare
> halls, just as it had been once, communities
> beleaguered but the closer
> the intenser for it, with resources

now distributed to need, and organised to last,
the dance floors stacked
with foodstuffs like a dockside, as if
an atavistic common memory, an inheritance
perhaps long thought romantic,
like the old men's proud and bitter
tales of 1926, was now being learnt again
in grandchildren and
great-grandchildren of their bloodline. . .'

Thatcher's Britain is a different country from the one I returned to in 1974. Extremists, whether they be Scargills, Benns, Norman Tebbits or Margaret Thatchers may, in opposition, play a valuable part in the evolution of society. But, given power, such fanatical ideologues as these tend to smash all that is fragile. Embattled as they are, they see enemies everywhere; they use the language of the lunatic asylum and speak, for instance, of 'The Enemy Within'.

Once, as a result of the Falklands War, Neil Kinnock called Margaret Thatcher 'bloodthirsty'. Afterwards he apologized. And so he should have done – for not being subtle enough.

One thing unchanged since 1974 is the operation of the literary mafia. As usual we are having those lists – The Best Books of 1984 – that permit some of my best friends to give a puff to some of my other best friends. Most of the books of poems recommended are boring, most of the novels lousy, most of the non-fiction not worth a candle.

My guess is that the best novel published in Britain during 1984 was one I happened on in Princeton in 1974: *The Wife of Martin Guerre* by Janet Lewis. It is a minor classic. When I returned home I recommended it to several publishers without success. Last summer Penguin published it. No madam, no sir, I do not know Janet Lewis.

I think the best short short story I read during 1984 was a feminist one. It concerns Beruriah and can be found in the Agoda of the Babylonian Talmud. It seems that Rabbi Jose met Beruriah walking on the road. 'Which way to the city of Lud?' asked the Rabbi. And Beruriah replied, 'You Galilean fool, don't our sages say, don't talk too long with a woman. You should have asked me, "Which way to Lud?" '

The best parable I came across in 1984 was one related in a lecture by Richard Ellmann who declared it was much loved by James Joyce. It is about an old man who, earlier this century, lived in the Blasket Islands (off the South West coast of Ireland) and who had not even visited the mainland.

One day he did so and, at a bazaar, came across a small hand-mirror – something he'd never seen before. He looked at it with wonder. He stared at it, stared again, then muttered softly, 'Oh father, father!' Seeing how much poignant pleasure he received from gazing into this small looking-glass they let him take it away. Now and then he would take it out of his pocket, stare into it, smile and say, 'Father.'

Then he rowed back to the Blaskets, jealously guarding his precious possession, and would not show it to his wife who became suspicious. What did he have in his pocket?

One hot day when they were both working in the fields, he hung his jacket over the hedge. She then took her opportunity to pull the object out of his pocket and gazed at it curiously. 'Ach,' she cried, throwing it away, 'it's only an old woman.'

My last patient at the chest clinic this year seemed to be more interested in his piles than in his chest. I told him how Galen, in the 2nd century, had treated anal bleeding. 'With a stone of India,' I continued, 'worn at the neck, an emerald in the navel and a black leg of a toad tucked under the armpit.'

'You're jokin', doctor,' said my patient.

Perhaps I was. After all, there are those who speak secrets they do not know, nor are they aware they have spoken them.

Abse's
1985

March–April 1985

It seems much more than three months since I looked out of the bedroom window and the leprous snow on the London pavement, on hedges, front garden lawns, trees, rooftops, hurt my eyes intolerably. I was ill. I drew the noise of the curtains and went back to bed, closed my eyes. I had never suffered a headache like this. Headache, photophobia, fever. Surely not a meningitis? No neck rigidity, so perhaps it was merely a severe influenza with meningism, an irritation of the meninges, the coverings of the brain, rather than a frank inflammation of these?

I stayed behind my eyelids and eventually fell asleep, woke, half-dreamed, blanks, slept, woke, headache, turned my head towards the wall because even the light breaking through the barrier of the drawn curtains bruised my eyes. I wished I could fall asleep properly, deeply, refreshingly, wake up free of this unrelenting headache.

Next morning I felt no better. I sat up in bed while Joan took my temperature. 101. It would probably climb higher by the evening. 'I'd better call Dr Ross,' Joan said. I dissuaded her. I told her the diagnosis: not meningism merely, but a viral meningitis or, as the textbook called it Benign Lymphocytic Meningitis. Where the hell had I picked up the virus? Headache, photophobia, fever, anorexia. Turkey? No, that visit had been several months ago. How long did meningeal viruses take to incubate? I wondered, too, if that episode, early in the new year, when I had rescued a mouse from Caitlin's soft pawings had significance. One medical authority curiously suggested that mice may harbour viruses that can cause meningitis. But I had simply banished the cat to the

89

living room, opened the door of the kitchen, and with a brush, gently, guided the shocked mouse into freezing 1985.

'It can't be TB meningitis,' I said to Joan. 'I've seen too many TB patients over the years. I must be resistant to TB. It's a viral meningitis.'

'Let's see what Dr Ross says,' Joan advised.

What was the point? There was no specific treatment for viral meningitis. Ross would come, would take my temperature, perhaps test my reflexes, then admit me to hospital. There they would extract a cubic inch or so of my cerebro-spinal fluid (a lumbar puncture) and send the fluid which would be as clear as gin to the laboratory and, after weeks, the diagnosis of benign lymphocytic meningitis would be confirmed. They called the condition benign because patients almost always survive it. It didn't *feel* benign. Headache, photophobia, dreaming blanks, time passing, analgesics, darkness, light, darkness, fever, analgesics.

Several days later Joan called in Dr Ross because, if anything, I was worse. After he'd examined me, listened to my short story of symptoms, Ross said, 'You'll have to go to hospital. What about the Royal Free in Hampstead? That's the nearest.'

'I don't fancy a lumbar puncture,' I grumbled.

In addition I did not want to lose Joan's sympathetic and tactful care – to exchange that for the more impersonal concern of hospital routine.

'There's only one place for you,' insisted Ross. 'Hospital. I know the neurologist at the Royal Free. He's first class. I'll telephone him now.'

Soon enough I lay in bed in a darkened emergency room at the Royal Free – the temperature high, the punishing headache and photophobia unchanged. One of the nurses said, 'Could you manage to walk down to the X-ray Department by yourself for a brain scan and chest X-ray? I could get a porter to wheel you there, but that may take a long time as we're so short-staffed.' (Did you hear, Mrs Thatcher?)

It was a long walk to the X-ray Department. Eventually I arrived, handed in a slip of a form, waited with the other haggard-looking patients on long benches and recalled how Plato had believed that the best doctors were those who had experienced disease themselves. Later I was wheeled back to a room which had again been darkened and listened through my headache to a patient next door who kept on shouting out terrible cries in a language I could not understand.

Eventually I was seen by the neurologist who believed the diagnosis to be Benign Lymphocytic Meningitis. A lumbar puncture was done and I didn't enjoy it at all. Ten days later my fever seemed to have abated and I asked them all to allow me to go back to the care of my wife who could make for me 'some very special Welsh tomato soup which was absolutely essential for my full recovery!'

When I returned home my temperature also returned. I had hoped to sit quietly in the armchair in the bedroom, listening to the radio, perhaps feeling better each day. When I was released from the Royal Free the consultant neurologist had said, 'It'll take some time for you to be fully recovered. You'll probably get depressed. Don't worry, that's a normal sequel to a meningitis. And don't go and see a psychiatrist. Just come to my outpatients. OK? Mind you don't get a relapse once you leave here.'

But that's what happened: a relapse. I lay in bed again – headache, photophobia, dreaming blanks, time passing, occasional visitors, Dr Ross, darkness, light, day, night, fever, and always Joan on call, near and kind and reassuring.

A true scientist would have listed his symptoms in precise detail, not impressionistically as I have done. Perhaps I should have followed the example of that great neurologist and first modern experimental gerontologist, Charles Brown-Sequard. He remained a scientist even to his last days in 1894 when, stricken with a right-sided haemorrhage of the brain, he continued to itemize precisely his own symptoms, correctly diagnosing his illness and its bleak prognosis – as if he were observing another patient. The next day he was dead.

At least I should have heeded the comment of my friend Sigi Nissel who is the second violinist of the Amadeus Quartet and who, as a result, frequently travels all over the world. One day, during a game of chess with him, I said, 'Sigi, you must get so bored of hotel bedrooms and travelling, travelling all the time. So many aeroplanes, so many airports, so many railway stations, trains, car rides, connections, it must be boring. I'd be bored, fed up to here.'

'I'm never bored.'

'C'mon. Never?'

'Never. Never. I used to get bored. But not for some years now.'

'You must let me into your secret,' I said cynically.

He hesitated. 'You don't know this,' he continued, 'but some years ago I had a brain tumour. I was operated on. In the event it proved to be a benign growth and I was left with no residual symptoms. Since then I'm never bored. I can play music and I can travel. I'm just grateful for each day.'

Chastened, I returned my gaze to the chessboard, listened to the silence, then moved a pawn.

I should be grateful too. I have not experienced any depression such as the neurologist at the Royal Free prophesied. For a couple of weeks I had been worried whether the cerebral nerves were affected. I had a toothache, jawache, then an earache and finally some difficulty in focusing my eyes properly. But all these symptoms passed. I'm back to my old routines of working in London at the chest clinic on Mondays and Tuesdays, returning sometimes to Ogmore, reading, playing chess, and as a matter of fact I am now having a particularly productive period of writing poems. So all's well and all manner of things.

Today I walked past my Uncle Joe's house and saw the notice outside: TO BE SOLD. Injurious Time. Strangers will come to live there and his name on the brass plate, Dr Joseph Shepherd, will be scandalously removed. In future, when I walk this way, I know I shall not cross the road with averted eyes but hesitate. And all deaths remind one of one's own:

> Ay, but to die, and go we know not where;
> To lie in cold obstruction and to rot;
> This sensible warm motion to become
> A kneaded clod; and the delighted spirit
> To bathe in fiery floods, or to reside
> In thrilling region of thick-ribbed ice;
> To be imprison'd in the viewless winds.
> And blown with restless violence round about
> The pendant world; or to be worse than worst
> Of those that lawless and uncertain thoughts
> Imagine howling: 'tis too horrible!

Of all my uncles and aunts who have departed this world to become speechless and disgraced, I miss Joe the most. Had he been alive when I had my viral meningitis he would certainly have been summoned to my bedside. He was a most skilled GP. A physician who, unlike so many others, kept up to date with medical advances and who, besides, read widely in disciplines other than medicine.

Over the years I referred a number of patients to him, including a few poets and their wives. I think Joe delighted in having slightly off-beat patients. Most of them were well-heeled, living locally, but he also treated a number of working-class Irishmen. 'Why do you have so many Irishmen from Kilburn coming to you, uncle?' 'Word of mouth,' he would reply before telling me a riveting anecdote about one or another of them. One story he told me was surely material for a Zola or a Guy de Maupassant. It concerned a short-statured, wiry Irishman who, Joe decided, needed an abdominal operation.

Patrick, sitting up on the couch, after the clinical examination, said, 'Well, if you think it desperately necessary, doctor.' The patient then asserted that he wanted the operation to be done privately. He was not interested in the National Health Service. Joe, believing that his patient could ill-afford private surgery, tried to dissuade him.

'Money's no object,' declared Patrick. 'Sure, it's no problem at all. I want the best and most corrigible surgeon in the land.'

Joe, curious now about the apparently limitless wealth of his patient, expressed surprise that plumbing was such a lucrative business. Patrick looked discomforted. He cleared his throat. At length he asked, 'You've taken the solemn oath, haven't you, doctor, like all doctors? Whatever I say here is entirely confidential, isn't it?'

Joe assured him that this was so, then his patient admitted, 'I'm not a plumber, doctor. I told you a lie. That was the heart of falsehood. I'm a burglar.'

My uncle, poker-faced, recommended the noted surgeon, Dickson Wright of St Mary's Hospital, to undertake the operation. 'I'll phone him right away,' Joe said. Patrick nodded and my uncle turned the pages of the Medical Directory seeking Dickson Wright's home telephone number. Before dialling it, he repeated the number out loud and his patient cried, 'Dija say

Cunningham? A fig! Is it a Cunningham number? Why be damn, that's St John's Wood, isn't it? My beat's St John's Wood.'

'Your beat?'

'My practice, doctor. It's agreed between us. We do not trespass on each other's territory. What road does this surgeon live in?'

When Joe told him the street his patient stood up as if affronted. When he told him the number of the house Patrick said, 'I only did him two weeks ago. I've still got his pestilent stuff.'

Joe telephoned Dickson Wright. Yes, he had been burgled recently and yes, he had lost a lot of silver and how did Joe know?

'Do you want all your property returned?' asked Joe. 'Because if you do you'll have to operate for free.'

And so it came to pass . . . Patrick left St Mary's Hospital a healthier man and Dickson Wright had all his silver returned. I wish I could continue Joe's story by writing, 'Soon after – long enough for a man to convalesce from an abdominal operation – Dickson Wright's house was burgled again,' but such an addendum would, alas, belong to the lying vice of fiction.

May 1985

It is common practice nowadays to sell books at poetry readings. Organizers provide a table and ask the poet to bring books with him. Ordering such books, direct from a publisher, can be tricky. For instance, I telephone Tiptree where Hutchinson keep their warehouse. 'My name is Dannie Abse. I've ordered books from you before. May I have another sixty copies of my *Collected Poems* please?'

'That's ABSE, isn't it?'

'Yes.'

And you want *The Collected Poems*?'

'Right.'

'What's the name of the author?'

'Dannie Abse.'

'You want six copies of *The Collected Poems of Dannie Abse*.'

'Sixty copies.'

'Just a minute.'

I hold on. I wait until the voice returns. 'OK, now what is it you want?'

Three weeks later a parcel arrives from Tiptree. I open up the box and inside it I discover sixty copies of *The Collected Poems* . . . of Kingsley Amis! On the telephone I seem to have difficulty in making myself understood. When I demand that they take back Mr Amis's box when they deliver the sixty copies of *my Collected Poems*, they argue that that cannot be done. 'We only deliver, not take back.' I settle for them sending me sixty copies of my book and privately decide to return the Kingsley Amis volumes to the Editorial Department at Fitzroy Square. This I do, though heavy is this light-weight poet to carry, and eventually the second box of books arrives at my home from Tiptree. They have come too late for the poetry reading; no matter, there will be other readings and I open up the box in the hall. Soon I'm shouting, 'Joan. Joan, for Chrissake, come and look at this.' Tiptree have sent me sixty copies of *The Collected Poems* of the Pope.

Because we are all different, because we are not clones, because we all react differently in some measure to the assault of diseases and drugs, medicine is not a science, it cannot be. It has to rely on generalizations, not on laws. Not only are we not identical, but the germs that attack us are also individual. It has been said that there are as many B coli germs in the intestines as there are stars in the sky and under an ordinary microscope these bacteria appear to be the same. But a more sophisticated scrutiny, through an electron microscope, proves otherwise.

I've sent in my new book of poems to Anthony Whittome at Hutchinson today. It contains work over five years. I've called the book, *Ask The Bloody Horse* because I don't know and I still don't know where I'm going. I should have liked to put, as an epigraph, a quotation by Martin Buber: 'All journeys have secret destinations of which the traveller is unaware.' Alas, Charles Causley has done exactly that in one of his volumes. Instead I have prefaced the book with:

> While Freud was tracing the river to its source
> he met Itzig unsteadily riding.
> 'Where are you going?' he asked that wild-eyed rider.
> 'Don't ask me,' said Itzig, 'ask the bloody horse.'

Simply I've adapted the old joke about the novice horseman Itzig. Apparently it was Freud's favourite joke, presumably because he perceived the horse to be an emblem of the unconscious and recognized the truth of Itzig's response. Hence I introduced Freud into the quatrain. The best jokes, I think, often turn out to be humorous parables. Anyway, what is writ, is writ – Would it were worthier!

Fraser Steel has invited me to contribute to the *Poet on Poet* Radio 4 series he is producing. I was tempted to recycle the lecture I gave at the Poetry Society – *The Dread of Sylvia Plath*. On second thoughts, I decided to be less lazy. I have let Fraser know that I will write a piece on D. H. Lawrence. I've chosen Lawrence because I think that, generally, he is still underestimated as a poet.

Years ago, when I was a medical student, I happened on his poems for the first time and responded at once to 'The Ship of Death' and 'Bavarian Gentians'. I did not know then, being untutored, that these poems were among his last, were by a man dying of pulmonary tuberculosis. Re-reading these poems, aware of the fact, I find I am even more deeply touched now than I was then.

What a double-streaked man Lawrence was. His poems reveal it over and over again – at one moment he's gentle and patient, at another he is shrill, irascible. He was ambivalent about so many things, not least sex. That's why I like that early poem of his, one that critics do not much remark upon, and which begins, 'She said as well to me: Why are you ashamed?. . .' That poem not only shows, dramatically and precisely, Lawrence's ambiguous sexual preoccupations but articulates, characteristically enough, his vivid awareness of the mystery and, indeed, divinity of life – human and non-human life. When Keith Sagar writes, 'His vision becomes increasingly sacramental,' it is not entirely true. It is there from the beginning in the earliest poems, blurred, myopic, as in such bad poems as 'Mystic Blue' – the secretive, living dark (its blueness) was there then but abstract, not wonderfully concrete as the dying Lawrence was later to order it in 'Bavarian Gentians'.

I was about to leave the Tate Gallery when Mark Gertler's painting 'Merry-Go-Round' made me hesitate. It intrigued me: the background of night, the tense, open-mouthed wooden figures in the artificial light whose enjoyment, if it were such, was akin to that of spectators at a horror film. Gertler painted it in 1916 and no doubt was making some allegorical statement about the First World War.

On the way home I kept thinking of Gertler's painting, its ambiguity, the terror in it, and then I recalled Rilke's poem about a Merry-Go-Round at night. How typical, I thought, of Rilke to focus on such an image, interested as he was in the mediation of the invisible into the visible. ('The Angel of the Duino Elegies,' he wrote, 'is the being who vouches for the recognition of a higher degree of reality in the invisible, terrible to us because we . . . still cling to the visible.') Yes, the Merry-Go-Round at night was a given metaphor for Rilke: fairground spectators have the optical illusion of night's invisible creatures becoming tangible, as the roundabout turns them from darkness into light.

It was years since I had read Rilke's poem. When I arrived home I picked out Rilke's poems from the bookshelf. I read J. B. Leishman's translation of Das Karussell (I have no German, alas) and was astonished to discover I had misremembered the poem, that the Merry-Go-Round Rilke portrayed was not even one revolving at night! Somehow I must have merged Gertler's vision with my own weak remembrance of Rilke's poem. Doodling, I sat down to write the translation I thought I had remembered:

> The roof turns, the brassy merry-go-round crashes
>   out music. Gaudy horses gallop tail to snout,
>   inhabit the phantasmagoria of light
>   substantial as smoke. Then each one vanishes.
>
> Some pull carriages. Some children, frightened, hold tight
>   the reins as they arrive and disappear

chased by a scarlet lion that seems to sneer
not snarl. And here's a unicorn painted white.

Look! From another world this strange, lit retinue.
A boy on a steer, whooping, loud as dynamite –
a sheriff, no doubt, though dressed in sailor-blue.
And here comes the unicorn painted white.

Faster! The children spellbound, the animals prance,
and this is happiness, this no-man's land
where nothing's forbidden. And hardly a glance
at parents who smile, who *think* they understand

as the scarlet lion leaps into the night
and here comes the unicorn painted white.

The red-haired woman, with her fiancé lingering a yard behind,
approached me. It seemed she had once been in a BBC schools
programme I had conducted. Her fiancé nodded. 'I was only
fifteen then,' said the redhead.

So were all the other schoolchildren. I remembered the
occasion well because my own daughter, Susanna, took part in
the programme. The scheme was that I would read a poem of
my own choosing, one, say, by Hardy, or by Ted Hughes, and
afterwards the youngsters would comment, pronounce on why
they liked the poem or disliked it. The producer, Stuart Evans,
commanded, 'You will act as an active chairman,' and I asked if
Susanna could join the group for if she did so I knew there would
be no awkward, accumulating silences in the studio.

'But she's older than fifteen, isn't she?' asked Stuart.

'No,' I said, 'she's fifteen, a mature-looking, lipsticked fifteen,
but fifteen nevertheless.'

Stuart agreed, providing no one knew that I was her father. 'It
wouldn't be fair to the others if they knew,' he argued. So in due
course, anonymously but loudly, Susanna joined the schoolboys
and girls in the studio, including apparently this red-haired lady
who now stood before me. After the programme, Susanna had
hung back until all the others had departed, then I drove her
home, saying, 'I think it went quite well, don't you?'

'Fine,' Susanna had replied, 'but all the other kids thought
you were very peculiar, Dad.'

'Peculiar?' I said, mortified.
'Well, you did keep winking at me all the time.'

Memory. Proust was right when he averred that most of our days are forgotten, unremembered, and could be stored, as it were, in a book for some vast library, in a book that no reader will ever ask for, that will never be taken down.

July 1985

Dear Norman,
I read your poem about triangles with interest. Perhaps you should allow it to be part of a geometric sequence? In exchange, Norman Kreitman, I offer you this Diagram to Explain Religion:
Draw a large circle not quite complete. Allow two apertures, each a centimetre wide, east and west, for exits and entrances. Within, sketch houses, trees, gasworks, grass. Also scrupulous soldiers bayoneting each other. Above these, trapeze artists. Above these, vultures. Above these, clouds. Above these, aeroplanes. Also other creatures, other things of this world, leaving spaces, inches of whiteness, so that all that breathes may breathe.
Outside the circumference make no pencil mark, despite Old Masters who claimed familiarity with the shapes of angels, demons, dissident unicorns, etc. This is how it is. Sometimes, through the aperture in the east, sometimes from the west, the modest whiteness outside slips into the aerobic whiteness inside. Watch carefully. When you see this happen, when you see the differences in the white, then write at the bottom of the page that signature you once forged in Sleep's Visiting Book.
All that's good,
Dannie

Dear Francis Bacon,
Let me tell you something about that particular painting that has so influenced you, a painting, indeed, most seminal for many other contemporary painters.
I am in possession of a secret, one that I have never divulged before. Your master, you may recall, was slain by a coronary in the solitude of his studio the very morning he hoped to finish this masterpiece. What

you do not know is that the Angel of Death was about to leave softly, as usual, but he could not help gaze first at the canvas on the easel, at the contained black uproar on the canvas. With slow, such strange slow recognition, he stood there amazed. He bent down, excited, plucked the paintbrush from the recumbent's wax-work hand. He rose. Compelled, he approached the easel, completed the dark picture with hurried, moonless-dark brushstrokes. Note how this, the most melancholy, most macabre painting extant, remains unsigned . . . I take it you will not broadcast this secret. But having just been to your exhibition at the Tate I thought you would like to know.

As ever,
    Dannie Abse

The biopsy proved that President Reagan has an intestinal neoplasm. Hence the telephone call from the *Sunday Express*. The *Express* spoke with the voice of Lady Olga Maitland, that well-known CND basher and gossip columnist. I was surprised to hear from her.

Lady O.M.   'In January 1984, you looked into your Orwellian crystal ball and wrote in the *Ham and High* that President Reagan would suffer a bowel cancer.'

D.A.   'Mmm?'

Lady O.M.   'The first suggestion that the President had anything suspicious at all was after a routine medical check-up in *May 1984*. So how did you know? Have you psychic powers?'

D.A.   'Mmm.'

Lady O.M.   'How did you come to the conclusion he would suffer from a bowel cancer?'

D.A.   'I have a cat – we call her Caitlin. She told me.'

Lady O.M.   'Seriously. How did you fathom it?'

D.A.   'I'm not going to tell you. Why should I let you into my secrets?'

Lady O.M.   'Mmm?'

Dissatisfied with my response, (I should perhaps have talked about Reagan's frustrated sadistic anal drives which, through neuro-transmitters, led to mitotic changes in the cells of the mucous membrane, etc.,) Lady Olga telephoned my relatives to discover whether I was a true psychic.

Leo's wife, Marjorie, eventually killed the *Express* story. For when Lady O.M. telephoned her she snorted, 'Dannie foretell the future? You're jokin' – he can't predict who's going to win a match at Cardiff Arms Park.'

Since the *Express* phoned I've had a call from *The Times*. Now I sit by the telephone waiting for the CIA.

August–September 1985

Passionately held political convictions are likely to unhinge one who sets himself up as a literary critic, especially if he lacks a sense of humour. Certainly I was mildly irritated by John Barnie's review of *Wales in Verse*, an anthology I had edited for the Secker series. Despite remarking that it was 'an enjoyable anthology' Mr Barnie concentrated on attacking my brief inconsequential introduction rather than referring to the main text. True, he did focus on Anthony Conran's poem, 'Elegy for the Welsh Dead in the Falkland Islands, 1982' only to suggest, 'In his short introduction, Abse is at pains, it seems to me, to diminish the impact of a poem like this for his English readers.'

Why should I have wished to have done that? The poem is a bitter one, the only successful poem I know written about the war in the Falklands, and it so happens that I liked it not only as a poem but was, and am, in close sympathy with what is being said. My own view about the Falklands war is no different now from that which I expressed at the time in *Authors Take Sides on the Falklands** when, along with others, in that summer of 1982, I was asked: 'Are you for or against our Government's response to the Argentinian annexation of the Falkland Islands?'

Indeed, when Anthony Conran sent me his poem to read he made it clear that it was for my private perusal. He felt the poem, if published, might wound susceptible relatives of the Welsh casualties. I persuaded him otherwise and he allowed me to publish the poem first in *Wales in Verse*. I count that a privilege.

It needed a heart specialist, Dr Vladimir Gurewich, to point it out – that in paintings of the crucifixion prior to 1630 the wounds

* See Appendix 1

of Christ are always depicted as being on the right side of the body. But, in 1628, William Harvey published *The Circulation of the Blood*. A few years later painters switched the wounds to the left. An anatomy lesson for Rembrandt!

Letters from America indicate that my poetry reading tour next month will be alarmingly strenuous: as far west as Iowa, as far north as Chicago, as far south as Texas. It's the travelling I dread most. Apart from readings I shall be obliged to give a lecture or two at medical schools – the relationship of Literature and Medicine. I have given very few formal lectures and I suspect I'm not very good at it – though I was pleased enough with my Gwyn Jones lecture I gave exactly a year ago at University College, Cardiff.* That was easy. I read a paper, hardly the best way though, to entertain an audience.

Of course it is better to improvise, or at least seemingly improvise, like those lectures delivered, yes *delivered*, years ago by Dr Ernest Lloyd at Westminster Hospital when I was a medical student but which I still vividly remember. Ernie Lloyd resembled Lloyd George; he took him, I think, as a model, and even barbered his long white hair in the same fashion. Ernie did not wear a cloak but it would have become him. He would commence (not begin) his histrionic lectures on Cardiac Diseases by throwing out his left hand towards the ceiling, pause ceremonially, then with hand still elevated, stare steadily over his spectacles at his now curious student audience. Suddenly, he would shout in Welsh-English, as if announcing the Emperor of the World, *the heart, ladies and gentlemen, the old heart*. And slowly, inch by inch, lovely ham that he was, he would bring his left hand down until it reached his left chest where he would open and close it rhythmically as he continued, 'beats eighty times a minute, minute in, minute out, hour in, hour out, week in, week out, month in, month out, year in, year out . . . the old heart.'

After this prolegomenon he would lean forward as if to tell us some arcane, naughty secret. 'Have you ever heard a mitral murmur, boys, have you?' he would say softly. 'It's like the wind rustling through the golden corn. You think I'm being poetic?

* See Appendix 2

102

Why, when you listen with your stethoscope to the old heart, boys, you are listening to a kind of poetry.'

How many Abse family stories have I listened to over the years about cousins who played practical jokes on other cousins, (of hilarious invention, of course) of uncles roaring with laughter at the discomfiture of other uncles and aunts who had been benignly fooled by them? Perhaps playing practical jokes is in the Abse genes, a family trait, but ever since I read W. H. Auden's essay 'The Joker in the Pack' I have paused before assuming the role of manipulative practical joker. Auden argues that every practical joke has a sinister element, that the joker is not only interested in unattractive power but has an identity problem. Fearful of being a brummagem he can only cry out, 'I am' when he tears the mask from his face as he laughs at his put-down victim. 'The practical joker,' Auden writes, 'desires to make others obey without being aware of his existence until the moment of his theophany when he says, "Behold the god whose puppets you have been and behold, he does not look like a god but is a human being just like yourselves."

But I would argue with Auden when he continues, 'even the most harmless practical joke is an expression of the joker's contempt for those he deceives'. I don't believe that. For instance – this may sound a bald remark – I am full of admiration for my wife and yet, once every two years, I become a fully-fledged Abse and play a practical joke on her.

A few mornings ago I was presenting a pre-recorded *Poetry Please* on Radio 4. I could not turn on the radio for, at that moment, I was at the clinic talking to a patient who had contracted a yeast-like fungus lung disease while out in Arizona – coccidioidomycosis. However I knew that Joan would probably be listening to the programme so, after the patient left, on impulse I telephoned home to ask:

'Ees Dr Abs zere, plis?'

'No, I'm afraid he's not here at present', Joan replied.

'Ah. Uh. Ees that Mrs Abs?'

'Yes, it is. Can I help you?'

'Uh. Ah. I just vanted to say that I vos listening to *Poetry Plis* and I thought your husband vas Vunderful. *Simply vunderful.*'

'How kind of you to phone,' said Joan.

'Uh. Ah. You vill tell him of my admiration.'

'Certainly. Thank you.'

'And it's a vise vife, wouldn't you say, who knows her own husband, plis!'

Oddly, two days later, yesterday (my birthday), my brother Leo, wishing on my birthday to be fraternal, telephoned me.

'Dannie Abse?'

'Speaking,' I said, recognizing at once Leo's unmistakable Welsh accent, though for some reason he was trying to pretend he was a telephone operator.

'Will you take a reverse call from Ankara?' he said.

'Yes, Leo,' I replied.

Leo, who is now sixty-eight, told me that on the Friday he would publicly announce his intention to retire at the next General Election. This morning, September 28th, *The Times* is on my desk and I read Leo's speech: 'I have no intention of joining the ranks of ageing politicians who, Reagan-like, maniacally deny the ageing process and death itself. It is time to get a younger standard bearer in the constituency to give support to Neil Kinnock's premiership.'

It worries me that he speaks in such a resigned fashion; indeed my conversations with him recently are too much about Time passing and our eventual certain assignments with Thanatos. Leo has confessed in his book *Private Member* how the first year in the House of Commons was one of the most painful of his life: 'The nights after I left the Commons for my lonely hotel room were full of nightmares and terror: seemingly for hours I would, in a twilight world between dream and wakefulness be gripped by vertigo. The whole room would spin round me, now slowly, now like some ghastly merry-go-round totally out of control, and again and again my attempts to impose order and stillness on the whirling furniture would fail. I was unbalanced and had lost my bearings.'

I think leaving the Commons may be equally disturbing for him. After all, so much of his life has revolved around politics. He has been an MP since 1958 and before that he had been a Cardiff councillor. When he was twenty-one, before he had had the opportunity to vote himself, he had been adopted as a Labour councillor for one of the Cardiff wards. I was a fourteen year old schoolboy then and was soon chanting:

> Vote vote vote for Leo Abse
> Kick old Whitey in the pants.

Leo is one of the most remarkable individuals I have ever known. What startles those who do not know him is his proclivity to offer ceaseless Freudian explanations for argued beliefs or particular actions. It naturally upsets them! He has worn psycho-analytical spectacles for scores of years. When we both lived in our parents' house in Cardiff he had, pinned up on his bedroom wall, a reproduction of Giorgione's 'La Tempesta'. 'It shouldn't have been called 'The Tempest',' he argued. 'It's post-coital. Look how calm and serene the scene. The storm has passed; the man is dressed now and the naked woman is feeding her child. Look how between them flows the river which represents Time, does it not, flowing on to eternity eternally. And note in the foreground how the column is broken, a spent penis symbol. Right?'

Unpredictable, original, irritating, tactless, extremely efficient, quick to understand a problem and to suggest a sensible solution, it must have been vexing for him to have watched fellow MPs, less gifted, though more tactful, some associated with Cardiff like James Callaghan or George Thomas, achieve honours and positions of power while he remained a backbencher. Yet, as Michael Foot once said to me, 'Leo did more to raise the quality of life for many in Britain through his private bills than did the government under Wilson's long tenancy at 10 Downing Street.'

When Leo entered parliament, Aneurin Bevan advized him to 'cultivate irreverence'. Leo never needed that advice. On the contrary, a dose of foreign office caution might have been more corrective for him. But a man's character, of course, is his fate, and Leo, quite rightly, had to be and must continue to be, himself. He will continue for the next two years anyway to impugn overtly the motives of his fellow MPs, inform them, man to man, that their actions are an expression of auto-erotic narcissism or repressed homosexuality or – as he once said to a bewildered Richard

Crossman – 'The trouble with you, Dick, you're an obsessional; it's all to do with your early potty training.'

Leo's judgement of people, or rather his sometimes bizarre reasons for his prejudice for or against them, must make his auditor wonder. Not long ago I asked him what he thought of Robert Maxwell who, of course, years ago, had been a Labour MP. Leo hesitated. 'Didn't know him too well. But I didn't care for him.'

'Why not?'

'Well ... he opened doors for me. He'd rush ahead, right, to open a door, you know. By being so subservient he must have experienced a feeling of power. No, didn't care for him. Right?'

When Leo was elected in 1958, I met him soon after at the Palace of Westminster. He was wearing a polo-necked sweater and a suede jacket. He looked boyish, not like a dignified MP at all, nor had he assumed then the flamboyant clothes so character-istic of him some years later.

'How do you like being an MP?' I asked, as he led me into the deserted medieval Westminster Hall.

'I'm forty,' he said. 'Life begins at forty! One should change the direction of one's life at forty.'

As we stood there grinning, suddenly the chimes of Big Ben struck the hour clear and near. Nine times. We waited silently and Leo ceased smiling. 'You know,' he continued softly, solemnly, 'ever since I've been a small boy I've dreamed of this moment, to be standing here as an MP and listening to Big Ben chime like that. I've achieved my ambition.'

'Well,' I said, 'what next, Leo? Have you further ambitions?'

'No, no,' he said.

'Wouldn't you like to be a minister?'

'No, no,' he said with utter seriousness. 'To be a backbencher, that's all that I wanted. That's enough, that's all I want. One can, with luck, be of use as a backbencher.'

He seemed overcome. He did not speak further and I was moved because I could see he was moved. As we continued to walk together silently I recalled how Freud had achieved his boyhood ambition of visiting Athens, of standing before the Parthenon and had felt unaccountably depressed. Later he recog-nized the source of his depression – he felt unworthy, as if he had been guilty of parricide. I did not guess Leo's own uncertainties. He always appeared to be so confident, so buoyant. If I had had an inkling of his true state of mind I might have referred to Freud's paper. Leo then, of course, had not yet written *Private Member* in which he echoed Freud by writing, 'All achievements bring guilt, and those most yearned for in childhood, on attainment, bring the heaviest neurotic burdens.'

Leo is a superb orator. He has certainly been unashamed of high rhetoric ever since he first uttered in public. I see him now, twenty-one years of age, standing on the raised platform of the drab, small, misnamed Sunshine Hall in the district of Canton, Cardiff, addressing forty or so individuals in wet, smelly raincoats and pronouncing, 'It is given to man to live but once and he should so live, that dying he may say, all my life and all my strength have been devoted to the finest cause in the world: the enlightenment and liberation of mankind.'

I was fourteen years of age and thrilled to hear such oratory. Later, when I read poetry seriously I could see the relationship between such oratory and certain modes of verse. For instance, Walt Whitman:

Not a grave of the murder'd for freedom but grows seed for freedom,
    in its turn to bear seed,
Which the winds carry afar and resow, and the rains and the snows
    nourish.
Not a disembodied spirit can the weapon of tyrants let loose
But it stalks invisibly over the earth, whispering, counselling,
    cautioning,
Liberty, let others despair of you – I never despair of you.

Is the house shut? is the master away?
Nevertheless, be ready, be not weary of watching,
He will soon return, his messengers come anon.

Could this not have been spoken by some brilliant orator at a political meeting? It is as much oratory as it is poetry while remaining recognizably the latter. It breaks the rules of poetry: it does not crystallize, it does not avoid generalizations, it relies on abstract words like 'Liberty'. And like oratory, rational and lucid as its meaning is, the hypnotic rhythms needle their way beyond the conscious mind.

Donald Davie, in his essay 'The Rhetoric of Emotion' would have us believe that there is a difference between the rhetoric of poetry and that of oratory. The orator, he suggests, endeavours to provoke emotion in order to make his auditors act, whereas in rhetorical literature the emotional inflammation is the end in itself. This, no doubt, is true for many rhetorical poets, Swinburne, Yeats, Dylan Thomas among them, but not for others and certainly not for many of the contributors to the first anthology of poetry I ever read voluntarily as a schoolboy, *Poems for Spain*. That was a time when Spain was the bloodiest arena in Europe and many an honest man or woman was appalled by Britain's Non-Intervention policy. The poets, then, like orators, were telling us 'a future of dust advances' and were trying to persuade people to act.

Most poets in Britain now avoid such large-gestured rhetoric. So, for that matter, with few exceptions, do our members of Parliament. Their speeches are cliché-ridden, modest, atrophic, grey, and they conclude with 'At the end of the day.' I suggested to Leo that this is because they were not brought up on the Bible: they did not have in their bloodstream, as it were, the enchanting cadences and parallelisms of the King James's Bible, unlike the old-time orators: Lloyd George, Churchill, Aneurin Bevan.

'The majority of MPs don't read anything,' Leo said, 'apart from sociological and economic textbooks.'

Perhaps the eschewing of rhetoric by post-war poets and MPs is because of the distrust of demagogy. Rhetoric – Hitler, Mussolini, Oswald Mosley – had been put to unprincipled use. As Ferdinand Brunetière declared in the nineteenth century: 'Where reasoning wanders, and reason even blenches there does rhetoric come and found its empire. It lays hold of an entire province of the human mind, not the least vast and inaccessible, and impenetrable to the demonstrations of erudition and the inductions of metaphysic; it establishes itself there and reigns in sovereign sway.' Throughout history monsters like Hitler have known how to calculate the effects of their bacterial rhetoric.

Why did the poets of the 1950s, the Movement poets, opt for a neutral tone and a cool accountant diction? Was it only a dialectical contradiction of its opposite – the verbal strategies of Dylan Thomas and the then fashionable excesses of neo-romanticism? Perhaps it was also, unconsciously, a rebellion against the fashions of oratory – the age of Churchill was over and we had been led to the very edge of the chasm. Even the eloquent poets of that time seemed to distrust eloquence! Here's Emanuel Litvinoff, a war poet writing post-war – 'The Orator':

> . . . His rich voice sweetened on corpses.
> Deep and thrilling, he could meet their praise
> With lush and laurelled dignities, raise
> Verbal cenotaphs to close their violence.
> The brave thunder of his guns in war
> Shamed the inglorious reproach of grief.
>
> What did it matter if his metaphors
> Were frayed and mildewed like a sack of rags?
> He knew the magic of old spells could bind
> A power of hate upon his ancient curses,
> And he could patch and mend his purple cloak
> To prove the repetition of events.
>
> Walking in space he dread to touch the ground
> And lose his pain in commonplace commotion,
> Rather would he be a bronze bell ringing
> Carillons for victory and harvest or,
> Better still, toll the bruised silence
> Falling like ash on the spent field of war.

Yet when all's said and done, as Leo recently declared in a lecture at Oxford (he could have quoted Cicero), 'Rhetoric can inspire, persuade and finally move men into the cause of justice and prompt them into action that improves our lot and theirs.'

October–November 1985

Iowa City was a pleasant surprise: a river as wide as the Taff in Cardiff flowed right through the campus.

As Paul Zimmer led Joan and me into the hotel foyer we stumbled into Gerald Stern, a poet of some renown in the USA.

'Are you all right now, Gerry?' asked Paul Zimmer. 'I know you've still got a bullet in your jaw.'

'Yeh,' replied Gerald Stern. 'The surgeon decided to leave it there. I'm OK except that when I go through security at the airport the bells ring, the buzzers buzz and all the lights go on.'

Poetry Readings, it seems, can be dangerous in the USA. I have not heard of any poet on the circuit being shot in Britain though not a few perhaps, deserve to be. Gerald Stern was scheduled to read with Daniel Hoffman in Philadelphia. He had flown from Iowa City into Newark, New Jersey, where he had been met by one of the organizers of the prospective reading. Stern, very much a verbal man as I was to discover, perhaps distracted the driver with his lively conversation. Anyway, she soon lost her way. Newark, New Jersey, is not a good place to lose your way in. It makes Merthyr on a winter's night look like a garden city. As the driver hesitated at traffic lights, wondering whether to go right or left, a group of black youths appeared waving guns, demanding money. One of the youths, possibly smashed, without warning suddenly emptied his wild revolver and one of the bullets lodged in Gerald Stern's jaw.

'Hey,' said Gerald Stern lightly, 'I never made that reading with Daniel Hoffman but I'm coming to yours tomorrow!'

The lift, or rather the elevator, took Joan and me to our spacious room. I looked out of the window at this other America, so far from Newark, New Jersey. We could see the river. The trees were wonderfully rusted into colour - mustard, gold, brown, ochre, crimson – more spectacularly than they would be at home. One leaf fell slowly, as if on a stage set, and the river flowed on through the expensively-mounted opera landscape.

Rochester, NY. After our brief sojourn at Penn State, Joan and I temporarily parted ways. She drove the hired car to Washington, while I took a flight to Rochester where I was scheduled to give one talk and two readings over several days.

The first reading was to be at the medical school. So on Wednesday afternoon I was led into a large lecture room. Above me, row above row, sat medical students, a few doctors in white coats, other faculty staff. On the blackboard had been chalked: DON'T FORGET YOUR ANATOMY EXAMINATION IS TOMORROW. I decided that apart from reading poems relating to my own medical experience, it would be appropriate to read a page or two from my autobiography, *A Poet in the Family*, where I described my first reactions to working in the Dissecting Room. Those particular prose passages I had never read out loud before.

I had described how I had shared a cadaver with another nineteen year old medical student, one named Russell Barton, and how we had investigated that forlorn corpse, pried into its bloodless meat, dug into its sour formaldehyde-smelling material with our scalpels. The body we dissected seemed so anonymous. I continued, 'The neck, say, exposed with all its muscles and its vessels mimicking a coloured plate in an anatomy book seemed, soon enough, never to have belonged to a live person ... the hand, or rather the resemblance of a hand, had never held, it seemed, another hand in greeting or in tenderness, had never clenched a fist in anger, had never held a pen to sign an authentic name. For this thing – as the weeks, the months, passed by – this decreasing thing, visibly losing its divine proportions, this residue, this so-called trunk of a body, this legless, armless, headless thing had never had a name surely?'

My reading of this prose passage from *A Poet in the Family* called forth several responses from some of the audience. One doctor related how when he had been a student his partner in dissection could not bear to behold the corpse's face. When he was working on the body he put a cloth over it. Faceless, it was more anonymous. 'Guess what this student became?' said the doctor. 'A thoracic surgeon. When he operates he still does not see the face.'

A Catholic priest who had been in the lecture room told me that the previous year, when the Anatomy course was concluded, he arranged a service to be conducted at his church for the dead bodies that had been dissected. 'Because of that anonymity you justly spoke about,' he said. 'I wanted to put that right so I invited the students to come to the service and the relatives of the cadavers. Towards the end of the service I ordered the Anatomy attendant from the Dissecting Room to read out the register, one by one, of the dead. The names of the cadavers. Do you know, many of the students cried when they heard that plangent roll-call.'

In the evening I gave a poetry reading for the English Department and gave medical matters a miss. Some people from the town attended and one of them, when the reading was over, lingered behind until I was free. 'Do you remember me, Dannie?' he asked. He had an English voice. 'I'm sorry,' I said as I stared at the short, smiling, grey-haired man in front of me. He interrupted me. 'Why should you remember?' he said. 'It's forty years since we met. I'm in private practice here in Rochester. I'm a psychiatrist. My name's Russell Barton.'

Chicago. I was startled and pleased to see John F. Nims, the ex-editor of *Poetry* (Chicago) at the reading. He had once declared that 'poetry readings are to our time what the Black Plague was to the fourteenth century'. A letter of his had been printed in the Winter 1984/85 issue of the *American Scholar* in which he had quoted from Trollope's *Barchester Towers* changing 'Preaching clergyman' to 'visiting poet' and substituting 'poetry readings' for 'sermons'.

'There is, perhaps, no greater hardship inflicted on mankind in civilised and free countries, than the necessity of listening to poetry readings. No one but a visiting poet has, in these realms, the power of compelling an audience to sit silent and to be tormented. No one but a visiting poet can revel in platitudes, truisms, and untruisms, and yet receive as his undisputed privilege, the same respectful demeanour as though words of impassioned eloquence, or persuasive logic, fell from his lips. . . . A Member of Parliament can be laughed down or counted out. Town councillors can be tabooed. But no-one can rid himself of the visiting poet . . . that anxious longing for escape, which is the common consequence of poetry readings. . . . But you must excuse me, my insufficient young poet, if I yawn over your imperfect sentences, your repeated phrases, your false pathos, your drawlings and denouncings, your humming and hawing, your oh-ing and ah-ing.'

Nevertheless, there he sat, John Nims, demonstrating once again how for friendship's sake a man will suffer and endure many things. However, by now, living in Chicago with all those oh-ing and ah-ing poets passing through, John must have vigorous antibodies against the Black Plague racing through his bloodstream. Joe Paresi, who came to my other reading in Chicago (he's the present editor of *Poetry*), looked pretty fit too.

Philadelphia. After a long dream-like flight from Houston I was cheered at the barrier by seeing my real world again, for there, waiting, was Joan accompanied by Daniel Hoffman. Dan had arranged a reading for me at the University of Pennsylvania – Ezra Pound's and William Carlos Williams's student stamping-ground.

Next day, before the evening reading, suasible, we went with Dan and Liz Hoffman to catch the current Ars Medica exhibition: 'Art, medicine and the human condition' as it was importantly named. Well, St Luke is the patron saint of physicians and of painters. Tradition proclaims that he painted a portrait of the Virgin Mary and no doubt he practised alternative medicine.

A large section of the exhibition was devoted to Anatomy, a subfusc topic that does not usually preoccupy my thoughts but which, lately, I seem to have had a dose of. As I inspected 'Bloodletting Manikin, 1517', 'Removal of the Pia Mater and a Cross Section of the Brain, 1541', 'The Anatomy Lesson of Dr Pieter Paaw, 1615' and 'Muscle Man, 1739', I found myself imagining the onlookers at a 16th and 17th century public dissection. For at that time such dissections of human bodies were public ceremonies, specially sanctioned by the Church, and the invited spectators would have included priests as well as physicians and artists. Such an occasion was part of a festival, a kind of necrophilic Strip Show. Of course, they were also questing for the seat of the soul. After that failure, the festival would continue; actors would be called in to present a decorous play or musicians hired to play cathartic music.

And speaking of necrophilia, one of the most memorable images in the exhibition was surely Munch's 'Death and the Maiden' – a naked buxom lady dancing with an actively sexual skeleton. Haunting, too, was a woodcut by Munch, 'Visit of Condolence'. In the background a bed in which lies, under the bedsheets, a dead woman. To the left, close to us, a door has been opened by the widower, allowing entrance to visitors who have handkerchiefs held to their faces. They are not weeping. Rather it seems they are assaulted by the smell of the odious, but no doubt, well-beloved corpse.

How odd that is: in paintings, in prints, we are rarely directed towards an olfactory reality. All those beautiful painted flowers have no scent other than the paint itself.

November–December 1985

I was answering the letters that had accumulated while I was in the USA when the telephone sounded. It was Gavin Ewart. 'I enjoyed reading your piece in the *Poetry Review*,' Gavin said. 'That man, Norman Maw, I used to know him.'

In August I had quickly written a piece for the *Poetry Review* about a reading I had given in the Lake District and the behaviour of the, er, imposing gentleman who had chaired that reading*. Gavin was now puzzling me, for he continued to opine on someone called Norman Maw.

'Norman Maw?' I asked.

'Yes, your chairman,' Gavin said.

Only later, when I received the *Poetry Review* did I realize that Gavin's posh accent had changed Moore to Maw. Not that it made any difference: I did not know anyone called Norman Moore either. The description I had given of that Lake District reading was totally truthful but I had invented the name of the chairman. In fact, as I spoke to Gavin Ewart on the telephone, not only had I forgotten the name that I had invented, but I was even under the impression that I had omitted the name of the chairman altogether, leaving that gentleman anonymous.

'Did you say Norman Maw?' I asked.

'Norman Maw,' agreed Gavin.

'I don't know him,' I said.

'Yes you do,' Gavin insisted. 'So do I.'

I held the phone to my ear, feeling jet-lagged.

'Anyway, I enjoyed reading the piece – I just wanted to tell you that. And that I, too, know Norman Maw.'

'Norman Maw?'

'Yes, your chairman.'

'My chairman? Gavin, I didn't actually give the name of the chairman in that *Poetry Review* piece, did I?'

'Oh yes you did,' said Gavin. 'I have it here. Norman Maw. I could tell you stories about him myself.'

'But Gavin, I avoided giving the name of that chairman.'

* See Appendix 3

'Norman Maw,' said Gavin resolutely.

'I don't think it was Norman Maw,' I said.

'Yes it was,' said Gavin. 'It says so here in the *Poetry Review*. I knew him quite well. I was interested to learn that he's now living in the Lake District. I didn't know that.'

While we were in the USA our bright-eyed friend Hans Keller died. We shall miss him. As I'm writing this I hear his distinctive voice, his accent, the way he stated an opinion, one never tentative, utterly certain of its truth. Hans loved arguing, or to be more exact, 'fighting verbally'. Didn't he once remark, 'I am a fighter – but don't want to maim or kill anybody – which is a disadvantage!' He was remarkable in many ways – not least in that he could write a radio talk or a long complex lecture in his head. And then, when it came to its delivery, he only had to remember it.

Mozart, he told me, found the writing down of his compositions the least interesting aspect of his work. He was a clerk to himself and only had to remember his music and transcribe it. Mozart would listen, in fact, to other men's music while simultaneously he recorded his own!

Hans's favourite preoccupations were music, football and the theories and modifications of psychoanalytic psychiatry. In discussions of these subjects he was electrically alive. Even when he was quiet, when he carefully listened – often to the answer of a question he himself had posed – he seemed full of static electricity.

Brian Glanville once wrote that 'all goalkeepers are crazy'. By that, of course, he didn't mean they were psychotic. Simply, they tended to be more eccentric, more 'characters' than the rest of the team. Hans, when young, played football in goal – though remembering his wiry, matchstick frame which ever since I first knew him (1950?) had its Giacometti aspect, it was hard to imagine him punching out a ball from, say, a bustling corner.

At the BBC, where he worked for so many years, I'm sure he behaved rather like an international goalkeeper. Apart from opera he was in charge of all music. No doubt the BBC Managers had their problems with him. He did not want Radio 3 to become what it now is – a predominantly music programme. He was not in favour of cultural apartheid; he believed in mixed and contrasting planning. When Hans's views were labelled as eccentric, he replied, characteristically, with a question: 'In relation to which centre?'

He identified himself with the true heroes who took up maverick positions, like Freud, and who, at the time, appeared to be glaringly eccentric. He poured witty scorn on mediocrity.

In November 1938 as a teenager in Vienna, a Jewish boy, he was one of the victims of the Kristallnacht pogroms. He, like so many others, was beaten up, arrested, beaten up again, mentally tortured – on the sixth day of his imprisonment told 'Tomorrow at 6 a.m. you will be castrated and at 8 o'clock you will be executed.' He tells of these gruesome experiences in his one book which he entitled *1975 (1984 minus 9)*. A volume too little known. These experiences, I'm sure, left him with deep psychic wounds, but they also allowed him, as he himself asserted, the recurring awareness and grateful elation of being alive.

I think Hans overestimated my knowledge – I mean knowledge of a transcendental kind. He would ask me questions, metaphysical questions and he seemed to expect me to provide concrete, logical answers. Did he fancy that because I was a poet I was privy to certain supernal verities? I suspect he believed music itself was a secret language that had evolved over the milleniums from celestial discourse! Hans, as musician and critical interpreter, surely not only attempted to discover the names of the demons and of the gods, but quested, in a secular way, for what lay hidden behind the hidden, the revelation of the metadivine.

Now comes news of other casualties: Robert Graves, Philip Larkin, Geoffrey Grigson.

I met Robert Graves but once and I wrote an account of the meeting which I doubt Mr Graves would have enjoyed*. But I liked, and continue to like his poetry. He composed poems in the central English lyric tradition and he used a conservative diction and a logical syntax without display, though not without the power to surprise. His was an essentially romantic sensibility,

* In *A Strong Dose of Myself* (Hutchinson, 1983)

with belief in phantoms and miracle; in the terrifying and terrific supernatural; in his interest in myth as a surviving, operative power even in our so-called rational societies; and in his enduring preoccupation with the creative and destructive element that waxes and wanes in the man-woman relationship.

Indeed, almost one-third of Robert Graves's poems refer to this relationship. In 1963 he opined: 'My theme was always the practical impossibility, transcended only by miracle, of absolute love continuing between man and woman.' He seemed to believe in the mythographic story of woman as the lover and the destroyer of man. As Ronald Gaskill has put it – 'the story of man drawn inescapably to woman by her beauty, immolated in the act of love and finally supplanted by her son.'

Unlike D. H. Lawrence, Graves did not dwell on the physicality of man-woman love. With Graves one seldom senses a man and woman most and least themselves, coupling beneath the sheets. Rather we encounter the emotions of lovers or ex-lovers, and usually they are fully-clothed and courtly always, and civilized always, even in dismissal and disappointment. (Not surprisingly Graves called D. H. Lawrence a 'wretch', a man who is sick, muddle-headed and sex-mad). When we do discover Robert Graves's lovers in bed as in the poem 'Never Such Love' they are groping for words rather than for each other:

> Turned together and, as is customary,
> For words of rapture groping they
> 'Never such love,' swore 'ever before was.'
> Contrast with all loves that had failed or staled
> Registered their own as love indeed.

I hardly knew Larkin either. We met only at the Poetry Book Society committee meetings. As a chairman he was always courteous, always considerate, relieving argumentative tensions with humorous one-liners. He did not seem shy, though I'm sure he was.

In committee, he had a problem with his deafness. In earlier years he suffered, I understand, from a dire stammer. There was no trace of that handicap at the PBS meetings. Apparently that crippling stammer had dramatically cleared up when his father died. He was suddenly free to say what he wished. Yet later he suffered another kind of block. He could not write poetry.

> They fuck you up, your mum and dad.
> They may not mean to, but they do.

From all accounts Philip's father, the Coventry City Treasurer, had been a most dominating, authoritative figure, mercilessly tidy and solemn. According to Noel Hughes who had been at school with Philip Larkin, he, Sidney Larkin, went on visits to pre-war Germany and was struck by 'qualities of decisiveness and vigour in German public administration that compelled his admiration'.

Sooner or later someone will write a biography of Philip Larkin. My guess is that the biographer will not have to be a crude Jake Balokowsky to discover that Sidney Larkin was an unambiguous, fervent Nazi sympathizer.

How much did Philip model himself on his father? I do not mean politically, although Philip Larkin's own knee-jerk, right-wing views I find deplorable enough. (How absurd and naive of Craig Raine to write in today's *Guardian*, 'The nice thing about Larkin is that he was a reactionary.')

However much I admire Philip Larkin's poetry it was his social attitudes that made me feel distanced from him. It was predictable that when the PBS had to shift from the Arts Council's sheltering roof to either the care of the National Book League or to the Poetry Society, Philip supported the NBL because of its larger economic resources and despite its 'non-record' concerning poetry.

'I'm for the Big Battalions,' Philip argued, not being ironic, as of course Voltaire had been when he wrote, 'On dit que Dieu est toujours pour les gros bataillons.' The Big Battalions are what I've never been for. It's not for nothing that Cardiff City FC are now right at the bottom of Division Three!

It is good to be back in Ogmore. Because of the American trip we have not been here since October 6th. This time of the year one can take an oxygen walk to Southerndown without seeing anyone – for company there's only the sheep, the crows and the gulls, and perhaps an occasional self-absorbed, solitary dog. This

morning we took the sand route at first, for the tide was right;
then we climbed up and over the rocks to the high, breath-
holding cliffs. We observed a sheep utterly motionless. It seemed
to be reading a red danger sign on which was written
DANGEROUS CLIFFS. To mis-quote Shelley: there is only one
better walk in the world than from Ogmore to Southerndown
and that is the walk from Southerndown to Ogmore. The return
journey is especially good to take at dusk when one can watch
the slow Western mobile sunsets below the aeroplane vapour-
trails.

In the 1930s, when we lived in Cardiff, our car, a Riley, seemed
to know only one route. It would go instinctively to Ogmore-by-
sea. My father only had to sit in the driving seat, turn on the
ignition, and off it would go along the A48, up Tumble Down
Dick, through Cowbridge, up and down Crack Hill, all of the
twenty-three miles to the sea, the sea at Ogmore. Every half
sunny Sunday, every holiday, the car knew we wanted to play
cricket on the sands of Hardee's Bay while its boss, my father,
fished near the mouth of the river for dabs, salmon bass, and
ghosts.

Not only my immediate family homed back to Ogmore. Uncles
and aunts, fat and thin, cousins short and tall, from Cardiff,
Swansea, Ammanford, singing in their closed saloons, 'Stormy
Weather' and 'She was a Good Girl until I took her to a Dance'
returned to meet and quarrel and take a dip in the unstable
Ogmore estuary.

My sister, Huldah, once confided that she had lost her virginity
in one of the secret caves of Ogmore while my Uncle Max,
unaware, played the violin on the rocks nearby, and cousins and
their friends munched gritty tomato sandwiches and stared at the
incoming, loosely-chained sea.

Not everybody in the Abse family is stuck on Ogmore. I have
an American nephew, Nathan. When he was ten he came to stay
with us at Ogmore. His voice was inordinately deep and husky
and Virginian. He arrived after nightfall, gave the slate-black
emptiness of Ogmore the once over, heard the sheep munching
in the dark, then gazing towards the funfair's shimmering lights
across the bay of distant Porthcawl, said, 'Hey, man, let's take
off for civilization.'

I wish we could stay here longer. I'm fed up with driving up and down the M4, from and to London. But I don't see any solution to that. In the new year we shall still be making the same tedious journeys. No matter, now, as I breathe out the air of London and breathe in the air of Ogmore I know it's all worth it. I walk beside the cutlery-glinting sea, consoled by the sound of the waves' irregularities, by the pitch and tone of them, the 'sssh' of shingle, the way the sea slaps on rocks or shuffles sinking into the sand that sizzles as the tide recedes. And there, quite near really, the steamers pass, slow and hushed, around the breath-holding cliffs on their seamless way to the ports of Barry, Cardiff, Newport and, in dream, further, mysteriously, into 1986.

Postscripts
1986

January–February 1986

Both Joan and I have been reading Jeffrey Masson's book *The Assault on Truth*. Until given the sack, Masson worked on the archives at Freud's house in Maresfield Gardens, Hampstead. He discovered documents and letters which led him to write this rather scandalous volume.

Masson believes that trauma, sexual abuse or rape of a child by father or relative, lies at the root of most mental illness. This aetiological hypothesis Freud advocated in 1896 but discarded when he realized that his patients' rememberings of such assaults were but once-forgotten fantasies.

When Joan and I joined Carole and Jeremy Robson for an Indian meal our conversation circled around Masson's book, the details of which, particularly his description of the unnecessary iatrogenic, physical sufferings endured by Freud's patient, Emma Eckstein, had deeply shocked my wife. Indeed after the onion bhajis had been consumed, Joan and I were engaged in a too vigorous argument about Freud with the Robsons looking on, somewhat troubled.

Aware of their uneasy silence, I wanted to say to Joan in my middle class way, 'not in front of the neighbours, kid'. But her blood was up, as my mother would have put it. Thus, our verbal private aggression (assaults) continued until I, narked, found myself moving to a Hans Keller, barely forgivable, infuriating conclusion. 'I won't argue with you further, Joan, because 1. you are absolutely wrong and 2. because I am absolutely right.' I saw Carole and Jeremy simultaneously thrust their forks into their buttered chicken.

*

Paul and Susanna proudly visited us with their baby. More than a quarter of a century ago I had listened to Susanna's heartbeat before she had been born. A month ago, I put my right ear to Susanna's own tight, convex abdomen and heard the fast heartbeat of *her* child-to-be. I listened with a kind of muted excitement as if I had been privileged to hear the secret of the future. When I raised my head and could no longer hear that vibrant masterpiece the conversation between Keren and Joan continued. They were discussing the events in Northern Ireland and I felt as if I had plunged my face into ice-cold water.

Anyhow, here Susanna was with my first grandchild in her arms, the baby emperor herself. I gazed into her colourless, unfocused eyes. Her sight was still inward.

Paul told me that in April they intend to get married. They have been living together for several years but now it seems my son-out-of-law intends to become my son-in-law and they will make an honest grandfather out of me.

The Roll Call was to take place on Monday, February 17th, in the stone arena on the waterfront of the National Theatre from dawn to dusk. The names to be called belonged to some of the 10,000 Soviet Jews who had applied for and had been refused emigration visas. One name missing, fortunately, from that list would now be Anatole Scharansky.

When Tom Stoppard wrote asking if I would join one hundred or so others in reading a page of that register I had to accept. I had reservations, of course: I knew that many of these 'refuseniks' were religious zealots who, if they reached Israel, as was their imperative wish, would swell the numbers of those opposed to tolerant and more rational policies. On the other hand, I was aware, too, how, having applied for visas, these Jews, whatever their religious and political affiliations, were subject to arbitrary arrest, to searchings and to beatings, to all kinds of discrimination and harassment.

They had endured such humiliations for many years and were willing to endure them still, so how could one refuse to read for one and a half minutes a list of names to a microphone in the open air and to a TV camera on a cold February day?

I was sent a page to read. It began *Veronika Dubrovskaya*. And after her name was written the length of time she had been waiting for a visa: seven years. I looked down the list:

Rakhil Dulman – Seven years

Zinaida Kanevskaya – Six years

Svetlana Kaplan – Seven years

There were twenty names in all. So that Monday afternoon I left the chest clinic early and by 3.30 p.m. I was waiting with Brian Magee, Alan Sillitoe, Alfred Marks, Adrian Mitchell, and Sian Phillips, to take my turn and step forward to the microphone. Strewn on the stone arena in front of me were many carnations, more and more being added, each one representing a person who had applied for an exit visa and who was still forlornly waiting. The names of these individuals were read out continuously, one after one – a steady rhythm of names – for between, say Adrian Mitchell and Alan Sillitoe announcing their lists, elsewhere, over another microphone, other names were being called by drama students. One after one after one, regular as the beat of metronome, the long cast was identified, had been identified since dawn, and was still being called out now while, below, cold, the River Thames flowed on.

When it was my turn, I took the photocopied page of names from my pocket, walked over the discarded coloured flowers to the microphone and read out, '*Veronika Dubrovskaya* – seven years; *Fanya Dukhovnaya* – seven years.' And then, to my horror, I observed that somehow the photocopy print had, for some reason, become smudged so that the letters were out of focus and a number of the names quite unreadable. To fill up the gap in the list I quickly invented names. Did I say '*Alexey Karamazov* – eight years, *Ivan Ilyich* – seven years'?

I'm not sure, now, what Russian names I uttered, but soon the list became clear again and I was back to the real world of characters, not fiction:

Svetlana Kaplan – seven years

Yan Kaplan – seven years

Yuliya Kapustina – five years.

But what of the real names, half-erased, unreadable, that I did not call out? Who were they? Who are they? Where are they today?

*

It was a game, of course. Who, of all people in history would you have liked to dine with most? I did not hesitate long. Dismissing half-naked Helen of Troy, I plumped for Shakespeare. Yet if he spoke (no doubt eloquently) over our pizza, given his strong Elizabethan accent, would I have understood him? But think of the questions one could ask:

'Will, do you agree with Wordsworth that the sonnets unlocked your heart?'

'Mmmm?'

'How autobiographical are the sonnets?'

'Mmmm.'

'Can I have your opinion of the Earl of Southampton?'

'Mmmm.'

'Will, is that hair of yours a natural red?'

'Mmmm?'

'Will, during the plague in London in 1592 did you slope off to Italy?'

'Mmmm?'

'Will, Shakespearean scholars of today are very interested in the nature of your sexual appetites.'

'Mmmm?'

'Would you like a cappucino to follow your pizza?'

'Mmmm.'

I must stop day-dreaming. I agree with Stephen Booth's irrefutable assertion that William Shakespeare was almost certainly homosexual, bisexual or heterosexual.

March–April 1986

On my way back to the clinic I was startled to see ahead of me the doppelganger of a publisher's rep whom I used to encounter in the Welsh bookshop in Cecil Court. It could not be he for that rep had died several years ago. Frankly, I had never found him very congenial and as he, or rather the image of him, proceeded towards me I was surprised how he stared unsmilingly into my eyes as if awaiting recognition. I felt the cold at the back of my neck as he passed by silently.

Perhaps the wine taken over lunch, not excessive, had affected me more than I realized?

But sometimes, even the most sober of us and the most healthy of us, find it difficult to distinguish between illusion and reality. And not just man but the creatures too. If the Greeks are to be believed did not a certain stallion attempt to mount a mare painted by Appeles?!

What is real? What is not real? Hercules, startled by the lifelike quality of Daedalus's statue of himself, is reported to have thrown a stone at it. And when Byron visited Athens in 1810, his companion, Hobhouse, overheard Greek workmen refusing to carry a statue to Lord Elgin's ship for they believed they heard the statue sobbing at the prospect of exile.

But to meet one assumed dead walking down familiar Goodge Street at two o'clock of an afternoon does provoke feelings that are uncompanionable. The word 'uncanny' comes to mind. I suppose what makes an incident feel uncanny is when we can provide no plausible, mechanistic, *satisfying* explanation for it.

I find it interesting that the word for 'uncanny' in Arabic or Hebrew signifies also the daemonic.

We decided to dine out to celebrate the arrival of an advance copy of my new book of poems, *Ask The Bloody Horse.* We chose to eat at The Cosmo in Swiss Cottage. Joan and I had not visited that Viennese café for years but suddenly, in nostalgic mood, we wanted to make a return journey to 1949. In the post-war years, when I was a medical student, instead of studying in my 'digs' in Aberdare Gardens, NW6, Boyd's *Textbook of Pathology* or Hamilton Bailey's *Physical Signs in Clinical Surgery* I often spent an evening gossiping and arguing with other Cosmo habitués.

Because of the refugees who had come to live in small rooms scattered across Swiss Cottage, this area had become a corner of Vienna with a distinct café life. Soon, young British writers, artists, musicians and burglars, joined the refugees and found the party-going, cigarette-smoke laden atmosphere of The Cosmo congenial. Generally Joan – then Joan Mercer – and I sat in the annexe over one cup of coffee all night but there were occasions when the annexe was too full and its occupants overflowed into the large main restaurant where they had laid white linen table-cloths over the tables in order to encourage their clientele to eat something!

It was to the main restaurant that we now repaired. It had hardly changed. There was something old-fashioned about the place, something outmoded, as if the clock had stopped not so much in 1949 but in pre-war Vienna. On the walls were prints by Topolski and one had the feeling of not being in England. It was probable that the ageing waiters, despite their white coats, white shirts, black bow ties, were really chess players in disguise. The menu, too, was unaltered and surely unalterable, written down, as it were, with the permanence of the Ten Commandments. Thou shalt eat Rheinischer Sauerbraten with Dumplings and Red Cabbage or Wiener Schnitzel or Zwiebel Hockbraten or Zwiebel Rosbraten Viennoise, or Karlsbraten Veal Goulash.

The man (surely a successful refugee?) at the next table was already commanding his dinner. The waiter stood, pad and biro in hand, poised like a cat to spring on whatever sentence our next-door-table neighbour would utter.

'Uh-huh,' he finally asked, 'is it veal goulash?'

'Of course it's real,' the waiter said, baffled.

'I said veal not real,' he pronounced. 'If it's not veal I don't vant it.'

'It's veal, sir,' the chess player, disguised as a waiter, said.

'It's not pork?'

'No.'

'I don't vant pork.'

'It's not pork.'

'Pork I don't vant.'

'If it's written on the menu, veal, sir, it's veal. If it's written pork, it's pork.'

The customer once more read through the menu and the waiter waited.

'I'll have veal goulash,' he finally said.

It was odd to gaze around the restaurant and observe not one person known to us. Where were the novelists, youthful once more, Peter Brent, Bernice Rubens, Peter Vansittart? Where the sculptor, Bill Turnbull? Would not Emanuel Litvinoff, Cherry Marshall and Rudi Nassauer come in at any minute? Was Ivor M in jail again? Were Keith Sawbridge, Fred Goldsmith and Old Bondy next door in the annexe arguing the toss? I recalled Jack Ashman, somewhat manic, and Theodore Bikel with his guitar – and the prettier faces of Penny, Noa, Betty, Jacky, Peter the Girl,

Nina Shelley. I looked out of the window. Across the road where once had stood the elegant facades of fire-blitzed houses reigned instead W. H. Smith and MacDonalds.

Soon Joan and I were talking about the most remarkable ghost of The Cosmo, Elias Canetti. Canetti, some twenty years older than us, used to insist we called him Canetti, not Elias, since he did not care for his first name. But was that merely a rationalization? His own heroes, Stendhal, Kafka, Musil, among them, were hardly called, by us, Henri, Franz, and Bobby! He was a lord spiritually and lords have no first names. His unswerving courtesy, his evident erudition, did not diminish his formidable aura and presence.

Joan said, 'I wouldn't have dared join his table unless signalled to do so. He was so formidable. Of course, I was only twenty-three years old.'

Canetti would sit in The Cosmo regularly, often with pen in hand. When questioned on what he was writing he made it clear that it was a masterpiece. He had been working, he told us, on a book about Crowds and Power for more than a decade. When asked when he would publish it he quite seriously commented that there was plenty of time, that he did not wish to make the mistake Freud had done – contradict himself. 'I have to be sure,' he would say passionately. If ever a man believed he would one day receive the Nobel Prize for Literature that man was Elias Canetti. And he was right. Meanwhile we read the only book of Canetti's then available in English – his early novel *Auto-Da-Fé* – and we found it strangely memorable.

Joan, however formidable she found the middle-aged Canetti, did not think his conversation as remarkable as I did. Interesting yes, but not remarkable.

'Why do you find it *so* illuminating?' she had once asked me.

I could not, at that moment, quote anything particularly pithy. I recounted, instead, the story Canetti had told me the previous evening, about his meeting with Graham Greene: how Greene had expressed his admiration for *Auto-Da-Fé*, how he would be grateful if Canetti would sign his copy of the book for him. Canetti, it seemed, as he sat in his chair, observed a wall of books opposite him and noted how his own novel had been placed right at the bottom – 'Right-hand side, in the servile position of Z,' exclaimed Canetti. Meanwhile, as Canetti took in the insignificant, inferior, and therefore to him insulting position of his book, Greene scrambled about in search of it, up, down, right, left, centre, and though on his knees, could not locate Canetti's novel. And Canetti pretended he did not know where to look either.

'So what?' Joan had justly asked, after I had retold that anecdote.

I pondered. The story had depended so much on Canetti's own animated engagement with it as he had re-lived the incident, and how, with startling skill, he had mimicked Graham Greene's voice, mannerisms, posture, hesitations. In his telling of the story, Canetti had given his auditor a comical glimpse of a trivial power struggle, human rivalry.

'Next time Canetti says something wonderful,' Joan had said drily, 'let me know.'

A few evenings later, I joined Canetti at his table in the Cosmo annexe. As I listened to him, I realized how much I was impressed by the fact that he knew so many writers, had met so many whom I respected. Was I dazzled by the name-dropping as well as by his stunning erudition? It was more than that: he had the gift of making whomever he was with in conversation feel important.

> There is nothing so small but my tenderness paints
> It large on a background of gold.

He had the habit of holding his head to one side in a listening posture. He was acoustically aware, as most people aren't, to each word spoken, however trivial. 'Respect for others,' he believed, 'begins with not ignoring their words.' And so he listened to my youthful vapourings as if I spoke with the wisdom of Solomon. He paid attention as a great physician would. And he responded to a comment, to an idea proposed, often excitedly, vividly articulate.

Just before we quit The Cosmo at closing time – we had been talking about paranoia – Canetti remarked, 'But the man suffering from paranoia is correct. Someone *is* standing behind the door pumping invisible gas through the keyhole. For we're dying, right now, all of us, a little every minute.'

Later that night, long after midnight, when I went back to the flat in Belsize Square that I shared with Joan, she was asleep.

Soon I was lying in the dark thinking of Canetti's remark about paranoia and when Joan's regular, soft breathing altered I assumed she had woken up.

'Joan,' I whispered.

She stirred. 'You know what Canetti said,' I continued. She moved restlessly away to the other side of the bed.

'Canetti said,' I repeated.

'What?' Joan said, suddenly awake. 'What? What's the matter?'

'Canetti said that the man suffering from paranoia is correct,' I continued, 'someone *is* standing behind that door pumping invisible gas through the keyhole.'

The room was silent. Then Joan said, 'Christ, you woke me up, just to tell me *that*?'

Because of the publication of *Ask the Bloody Horse* Donald Sturrock has been making a short film about me for BBC2's *Bookmark* programme. Yesterday, when we had more or less finished this project, I asked him what writer would he be focusing on next?

'Any suggestions?' he countered.

I mentioned Canetti. At once I realized that that was a barren idea. Canetti would not allow himself to be interviewed on television. I suspect he would judge it to be too vulgar an enterprise. I recall how, during that Swiss Cottage period, he would express contempt for C. Day Lewis simply because that poet pot-boiled detective stories under another name – as if by doing so, words so legitimate in the confines of a poet's vocabulary, had somehow been sullied and betrayed. I think Canetti had an attitude towards words similar to that the Kabbalists once had for the holy Hebrew alphabet.

Once, in the Cosmo, I happened to share a table with W., an ex-Leavisite critic who had become a 'commercial' novelist and who had recently begun to contribute articles to the *Evening Standard*. After W. quit, Canetti joined me and passionately declared, 'You shouldn't talk to that man. He's worthless. Have you seen his articles, how he uses words? You'll be polluted by people like that.'

It seemed to me then, no less than now, that the notion that journalism could corrupt a serious writer was a romantic cliché and unlike many clichés, did not even encapsulate a truth. I know

I don't feel corrupted! Yet I continue to understand Canetti's concern for words – some would say abnormal concern. Words do seem to own divine attributes; one can believe they are the source of revelation and that if one could discover some secret combination of them one would attain eternal beatitude. They are like gods in a way, immortal and dangerous. We summon them to help us, to curse and to praise; they allow us some measure of understanding within them, and, beyond their definitions, there is only mystery and silence.

All writers are in thraldom to them and await word-attacks when sometimes, as if from nowhere, a poem results. If such given words do not arrange themselves coherently – I do not mean logically – then the artefact that results seems merely pathological.

Canetti has confessed to very odd 'word-attacks'. 'I recall that in England, during the war,' he wrote, 'I filled page after page with German words. They had nothing to do with what I was working on. Nor did they join together into any sentences. . . . They would suddenly take me by storm and I would cover a few pages with words, as fast as lightning. When I sensed that such a word-attack was imminent I would lock myself in as though to work. . . . I must add that I felt extremely happy during such a fit. Since then, there has been no doubt for me that words are charged with a special kind of passion. . . . They suddenly spring forth and demand their rights.'

To pack them into a mere detective novel then, or worse, into an inconsequential article for the *Evening Standard* was, for Canetti, surely to demean the gods themselves and to sell them into dark bondage as slaves.

I recall meeting Peter Williams in the infant's playground at Marlborough Road School, Cardiff, 'I'm six,' I said. He replied, 'I'm seven and I'm growing fast.' When I told him my name he told me his. Then he started boasting about his father.

'He knows everything,' Peter Williams said.

'Gosh,' I said. 'Bet he doesn't know my father.'

'Course he does,' Peter Williams said with the seriousness of authority.

'Go on,' I said.

'I'll tell you his name if you like,' said Peter.

'You don't know that,' I said.

'I do because my father knows him. He knows everything.'

'What's my father's name then?' I challenged him.

Peter Williams hesitated. 'Mr Abse,' he said. And I looked at him awed. Fancy having a father who knew everything.

When I went home and told my father that Peter Williams's father knew him my Dad said, 'Who?'

I related our conversation in the school playground and I couldn't understand then why my parents both laughed as if they were at the Music Hall.

I do not know why Peter Williams, aged seven, came to mind during the wedding ceremony for Paul Gogarty and Susanna Abse at the Registry Office yesterday. Perhaps it was because of my grandchild who slept through it all. The couple had agreed that Gogarty would be the child's surname if it were a boy, Abse if a girl. And now they were getting married the baby girl would still retain Abse as a surname. Her full name would be Larne, Kate, Gogarty, Abse. I like Gogarty as a first name. I can see myself calling her Goggers. But nobody in the playground when she's six will be able to fool her quite in the same way as Peter Williams fooled me.

May 1986

During the early 1960s I received the first note from one who signed himself 'The Master'. He had pencilled on a grubby half page, torn from a slumbering, green-lined exercise book, his peremptory message: 'I have just returned your novel, *Some Corner of an English Field*, to my local library. It shows greater control, tautness, economy than your earlier work; but you must ensure, in the passing years, that when you embark on writing prose it performs no disservice to the reputation of your poetry. Yours sincerely, "The Master".'

Who was this headmaster who patted me on the head? Wouldn't it have been more in keeping with anonymity if he had abused me? Called me upstart crow, rude groom, buckram gentleman, painted monster? I examined the postmark on the cheap, creased envelope: Beaconsfield. Who lived there? Disraeli had been dead these many years, so had the poet Edmund Waller. (I did not know, then, that Colonel Gadaffi's favourite spot in England was Beaconsfield. He had spent several months in England while a young soldier on a signals course.) So who of the 10,000 denizens of Georgian Beaconsfield had sent me that report?

Some months later I published a group of poems in a literary magazine and again the small office-brown shiny envelope with its postmark of Beaconsfield arrived. Within, I discovered the same grubby piece of paper, the same scrawl on it, the same signature and cognomen. Regularly, for several *years* after that, whenever I contributed to a magazine or broadcast on the radio or had a play produced, or published a book, I would usually receive a benign review from the anonymous Master of Beaconsfield. I did not welcome his unsolicited comments for I found his very anonymity disturbing but I had to acknowledge that his 'reviews' had a rare degree of percipience and, indeed, an elegance of style. His notes became letters and his letters were *composed*.

Then, one Saturday morning, I suddenly discovered who this wigged and stocking-faced Master was, for Joan happened to read a letter in the *New Statesman* by a certain novelist – or should I say, rather, an ex-novelist. And the address he disclosed was Beaconsfield.

'Didn't you used to know him?' Joan asked.

He was a novelist of the Thirties generation. When I had been a sixth form schoolboy in Cardiff I had read his contributions to John Lehmann's *Penguin New Writing*. Later, after I came to London to study medicine, I met him several times in the pubs of Soho and in the busy cafés of Swiss Cottage. Once, before I had published anything anywhere, he invited me to send him poems for a new magazine he proposed to edit. I did so and he accepted them. In the event, the magazine, to my disappointment never appeared and, oddly, he too disappeared – not only in person but as the years were to demonstrate, as a novelist too. Some time later I heard he had become a window cleaner and lived in Kilburn. Now, it was possible, he was domiciled in Beaconsfield.

'I didn't know him very well,' I told Joan, 'but he was

always kind to me. Do you really think he could be "The Master?" '

I decided to write to him – simply: 'Dear Master, I noted your address in the *NS*. It's been too many years since I've seen you. I trust all goes well and all manner of things. Best, Dannie.'

If he truly had been the author of those innominate letters he would not be baffled by my note. His response came quickly, the recognizable brown envelope, the tatty piece of paper. 'You are a very clever detective. I should have posted my letters to you far from Beaconsfield. The Master.'

That staccato note struck me as being very strange. One would have expected him, unmasked, to have been more chatty, personal perhaps, and certainly to have signed it with his real name. When I did not receive more letters from him, over the next year, I assumed that he felt no longer compelled to overlook my published work now that I knew his real identity. Not so; in September 1967, I contributed to a symposium published in *Encounter* called 'Intellectuals and Just Causes' which referred to the recent war in the Middle East between Arabs and Israelis. (Probably *Encounter* are organizing a similar feature, at present, following last week's Reagan bombing of Libya.) As a result of my contribution I received a shocking, anti-Semitic letter from 'The Master'. He praised Hitler and justified the murder of the Jews in Europe before allowing himself a more personal fusillade of insults. His letter revealed how deeply sick he was and so I had better not, even now, reveal his true name.

I ignored his sad, sodding letter and I did not hear from him again until 1974 when I published an autobiography, *A Poet in the Family*. This time he wrote at length, and blandly. After amiable comments about my book he dwelt on memories of his own early upbringing and adolescence. He concluded his twelve-page letter by sending me his best wishes and signed it once more 'The Master'. I thought, until this morning, that was the last and final signal from Beaconsfield, but among the few letters arrived by the first post were a few forwarded on to me from the BBC as a consequence of my short film in *Bookmark*. One envelope, brown, cheap, creased, which I opened proved to be empty. Had my correspondent simply forgotten to include the letter he had written? Or was this the ultimate in symbolic anon-ymity? I read my name *typed* on the envelope, c/o BBC and the original postmark – Northampton, a place as 'The Master' might have said himself, quite far from Beaconsfield.

I don't know. *I don't know.*

This morning (May 4th) an East wind was blowing so vigorously in Ogmore that our wooden gate had been thrust open. From the bedroom window I could see that a ewe with two lambs had trespassed into our garden. They were munching the daffodils and narcissi, a nice, forbidden, wicked breakfast. I rushed downstairs, still in my pyjamas, to shoo them out.

As I closed the gate behind them I thought more of the East wind than the sheep. Probably it was bearing invisible death-seeds from Chernobyl. Perhaps radioactive raindrops were sipped from the daffodil cups by the ewe and the lambs. Information, so far, is meagre. In any case, who can believe the complacent, stealthy, reassuring voices of experts and politicians? How much has been covered up before, how much will be told to us now? Will radioactive iodine be taken up by small, thirsty thyroid glands? What about my new granddaughter and all those like her from Ogmore-by-sea to the Ukraine and beyond where Prometheus is still chained to his rock while the vulture eats his liver?

Last Friday in Cardiff, I visited Llandaff Cathedral. I just happened to be nearby, so popped in as I used to as a boy, passing the yellow celandines beneath the yew tree. Inside soaring spaces of worship – Jewish, Moslem or Christian – I feel not just secular but utterly estranged like one without history or memory. Once more, numb, I observed Epstein's dominating aluminium Lazarus rising. And it was springtime, springtime in the real world and all seemingly dead things were coming alive again though a cancer sailed in from Chernobyl.

Inside the Cathedral, I ambled towards the Lady Chapel reredos where, on either side of the sculpted Madonna, six niches are filled with gold-leafed wreaths of wild flowers. In Welsh, dozens of flowers are named after the Virgin, as is proper in a nation that reveres the Mam of the family. The marigold is called Gold Mair – Mary's Gold; the buttercup, Mary's sweat; the briar rose, Mary's briar; the foxglove, Mary's thimble; the monkshood, Mary's slipper; the cowslip, Mary's primrose; and the snowdrop, Mary's taper. Tapr Mair.

If a man believed in a deity, any deity, goddess, god or God, he would, in that Cathedral, have prayed in English or Welsh or no language at all, for the neutralization of the death wind. And in Ogmore, this morning, as I stood in my pyjamas while the opera-dramatic clouds, grey, cream, or frowning darker, tracked so visibly westwards, my own lips moved.

And I wonder now, once again, as I move towards the close of this book, in the name of the God others believe in, how much longer will so-called civilized nations absurdly pile up unusable nuclear weapons and to what hell will Man be consigned if, accidentally or purposefully, radioactive winds sail in from places other than Chernobyl.

In our X–ray Department the radiographer, in the spirit of scientific enquiry, had gathered some rainwater and placed it on an underdeveloped chest X–ray film overnight to see if Chernobyl had arrived. He drew a blank.

'I left it too late,' he said, seemingly disappointed!

I think the Chernobyl accident will enduringly change perceptions of nuclear power, civil and military, yet no doubt people in Britain soon will cease to be intensely anxious about radiation dangers. They are, at present, much concerned. Several patients, this morning sent to the X–ray Department, were anxious about the extra radiation involved even in such a simple investigation as a chest X–ray.

After the morning clinic I had lunch with Tony Whittome, my editor at Hutchinson, to discuss the production of this book. We hardly spoke of Chernobyl.

'What about an index for the *Public Journals*?' I asked, aware how people browsing in bookshops sometimes read an index to see who was in, who was out.

I thought of those memoirs published a few years ago in the USA which focused particularly on the New York literati. In the index, opposite NORMAN MAILER, the author had mischievously had printed, 'Hi, Norman!' It might be fun to have an inventive index, I thought.

Tony Whittome related how Hutchinson had been sued on one occasion because of an entry in an index. 'We sent the manuscript out to the printer and, at the same time, delivered a copy to the lawyers for them to look over for libel. They advised us strongly to drop a name from page 182. A certain individual on that page had been characterized as a big gangster. So that man, maligned, became anonymous. Only we forgot about the index. Opposite page 182 there remained the villain's name, resoundingly clear and bold.'

I once asked my eldest brother, Wilfred, his opinion about a new book on contemporary trends in psychoanalysis.

'Am I in the index?' he queried.

'No,' I replied.

'Then it can't be any good,' he said with confidence.

Recently I saw my own name listed in the index of a volume about contemporary poetry: pages 66–67 I noted with some pleasure, believing that the author had devoted a couple of pages to my work. Alas, when I turned to page 66 I found the last word printed on it was *Dannie* and the first word on page 67 was *Abse*. The list then continued without further reference to me or my work. It turned out to be a lousy book anyway!

'No index then for *Public Journals*,' said Tony firmly.

'All right,' I said, 'but can I have a few appendices?'

I awoke at dawn and could not sleep again. I heard the bird-orchestra tuning up, one avian instrument after another. Closing my eyes I deliberately conjured up tranquillizing scenes. To that background of bird-rehearsal I turned on my own internal video of Ogmore-by-sea. This failing, I switched instead to Golders Hill Park.

I know no better small park in London, especially in May, than Golders Hill Park and after breakfast I walked there, past the empty bandstand towards the flower garden. I saw, then, how limited my dawn imagination had been – grey compared with these brazen colours. Beyond a bed of bold, uniform-red tulips, standing stiffly at attention, with dying daffodils in between, another plot, a whole military brigade on parade, hundreds of them, waiting for a brass band to strike up – yellow red, yellow purple, purple red. It was the pacific magnolia tree though, that rooted me. It spread horizontally, an epithalamion of full blossom with a few, just a few of its large, gorgeously creamy petals scattered on the paved pathway near my feet. Under the tree, a wooden park bench invited the visitor to sit and ponder. But surely no one would dare rest on it unless he or she were utterly beautiful, if not immortal!

As I hesitated, a blackbird alighted on a branch, half hidden by blossom, and began to play solo. I turned, then, wishing once more that I had the gift to praise, to praise more profoundly, before walking home, awake.

You ask me to tell you the end of the story. I do not know the end of the story. Mostly we collide with shadows. History itself is a public memory and like all memories unreliable. What should one person tell from the ant-heap but the intermittent recollection of his own days, and that, of course, only an approximation, a translation, a blurred tune on a comb, handwriting on blotting paper?

Appendices

Appendix 1

AUTHORS TAKE SIDES

The pure, pale criminal is one who admits to killing his victim solely because he enjoys the dramatic act of murder. For no other reason. Does he exist outside the pages of fiction? A real nice human-type murderer wishes to be thought of as sane, if not by others, then by himself. So in a gloomy cell he whispers to the Father Confessor or to the psychiatrist what he thinks to be the true cause of why he dismembered so bloodily his victim. The reason given may be momentous or apparently trivial: because, Father, the swine was possessed by the devil; because, doctor, the swine stole my wife; because, Father, the swine had treasure under the floorboards; because, doctor, each night the swine came into my garden and ate my gooseberries.

We who go to war, to patriotic murder, need for sanity's sake, a cause. The Greeks besieged Troy because beautiful Helen, they sincerely believed, had been abducted, forced into a coloured ship, that sailed for Troy. Yet there is another legend, another report, less sensational: Helen never went to Troy. She left home, yes, but not for Troy and she was not forced. She was elsewhere, Egypt perhaps, Cyprus perhaps, and those Trojans, those Greeks, slaughtered each other for ten long years because of a fairy story, a lying headline, a cloud, a ghost, an empty garment. I am one who believes this other story, that Helen was spotted by travellers on the banks of a delta:

Deep girdled, the sun in her hair, with that way of standing. . . .
The lively skin, the eyes and great eyelids,
'She was there, on the banks of a Delta', said Seferis

> 'And at Troy?
> Nothing. At Troy a phantom.
> So the gods willed it.
> And Paris lay with a shadow as though it were solid flesh;
> And we were slaughtered for Helen ten long years.'

We British are an aggressive nation. We seem to have become more violent this last decade: look how we drive fast and furious, with fists clenched; listen, at the stadiums, how the crowds shout, 'Kick his fuckin' head in,' or to the sirens of police cars and ambulances in the shoddy streets of Brixton or Liverpool. Listen to the usual thud of an explosion in Belfast. Most of the time, though, we turn our aggression inwards, we punish ourselves: we elect a leader who believes in Capital Punishment, who can punish us with conviction and with style, who with her male, public-school educated legions can sanguinely dismantle our Health Service, ruin our cities, pollute the air with lead or radio-activity, and make us unemployed.

Once we were told, 'You've never had it so good', and indeed we had never had it so good. It seems we felt we did not deserve it; our left hand was guilty; and our right hand was so guilty that we needed relief, we needed to be punished. But mother and Margaret, six of the best was not enough, is still not enough. We still have aggression to spare. We boil over. Ulster is getting boring; besides, there the issues are not black and white, they're complicated, confused. What we need is a clear issue. If we are going to murder anybody, God, we must have a clear issue, we must be *virtuous*. So what about a faraway island, one most of us have never heard of before – oh, don't tell us about treasure offshore – if we murder it must be for a pure principle.

No question, the Argentinian government are thugs in uniform. Yes, Argentinian thugs, who can deny that? It is true, it is documented. What a cause! What a Helen! So pass the drum, the gun and the blood-drip. Ta ra ra. Ta ra ra. Ta ra ra. (9 July 1982)

144

Appendix 2

UNDER THE INFLUENCE OF

I

I am told by scholarly critics, some of whom are presently anchored not too far from here, that Anglo-Welsh poetry is imbued with certain characteristics. These, it would seem, are derived from the Welsh language–literature tradition. No matter that the Anglo-Welsh poet cannot read the old language, that real thing strange; or that he does not even know translations of Welsh poetry despite the efforts of those like Gwyn Jones; the influence of it on his creativity, though he may deny it, is still active. 'Seepage' is the word our scholarly critics bandy about. The seepage 'on all cultural levels between the two language-groups of Wales' as Anthony Conran puts it.

Certainly it is a somewhat mystic notion that allows an Anglo-Welsh poet, ignorant of Welsh literature, to be most marvellously, most miraculously, affected by it. I do not mock. At least I do not mock with conviction because I know things can exist even when they cannot be invulnerably defined – like the concept of Welsh nationality itself.

In the introduction to the recently published *Anglo-Welsh Poetry 1480–1980* Raymond Garlick and Roland Mathias attempt to identify the idioplasm of the poetry they anthologize. The first ingredient they refer to is the 'inborn Welsh feeling ... that praise is what poetry should be about.' They argue, for instance, that when Dylan Thomas declared his poems were written 'for the love of Man and in praise of God' he spoke as a Welshman; in the same way, centuries earlier, when George Herbert asserted that a poet should be 'secretary of thy praise,' he was defining the Welsh view of a poet's function.

What Garlick and Mathias do not do is ponder on the relationship of David and Dafydd. After all, the Old Testament poets, when not uttering the poetry of curses, were also secretaries of praise. They extolled the Lord. They heaped praise on praise, image after image. Theirs was a most wondrous and rhetorical propitiation. Almost one thousand and eight hundred years ago the illustrious Rabbi Judah said, 'In our days the harp had seven strings, as the Psalmist has written: "By seven daily did I praise thee." ' Or consider the Talmudic blessing of the same century that is still sung over a goblet of wine at present day Jewish weddings: 'Blessed art thou our God, King of the Universe, who created joy and gladness, bridegroom and bride, mirth, song, delight and cheer, love and harmony, and peace and companionship. Soon the Lord, our God, may be heard in the cities of Judah and in the streets of Jerusalem, the voice of joy and the voice of gladness, the voice of the bridegroom and the voice of the bride, the jubilant voices of the espoused from their wedding canopy and the young people from their feast of singing. Blessed art thou our Lord who rejoices the bridegroom with the bride.'

Wouldn't that blessing fit nicely in Welsh? Or even uttered in a broader Welsh accent than I own? Doesn't it, come to think of it, sound like Dylan Thomas larking about, setting it up, in one of his prose pieces? When my grandfather, in 1887, was invited to preach in the chapel at Ystalyfera, when he uttered translated Hebrew rhetoric of this kind, David spoke to Dafydd, and the non-conformist congregation found neither the substance nor the manner of his sermon alien.

It can be remarked, cynically, that the praise of God was a somewhat amateur enterprise. The extolling poet had no guarantee of his reward: rain would not fall; nor was he relieved of his scabs and haemorrhoids. The Welsh bards were professional in comparison. Their praises, if laid on beautifully thick, were suitably rewarded by Prince ap Mammon. Sometimes the flattery was directed towards a lady but then, too, the bard looked for and probably received love's honorarium.

'The Song of Songs', which is Solomon's, the early theologians suggested, was religious praise-allegory. The second century AD rabbis, in order to include it in the canon, maintained that i signified God's love for the people of Israel. The Church Fathers of the same century, also finding the poem lush and alarming, interpreted it as being Christ's declaration of love for the Church. Nobody would imagine the Song of Songs which is Huw Morris's, to be allegorical. 'In praise of a girl' was in praise of a certain seventeenth century girl, praise of 'a slip of loveliness, slim seemly, freshly fashioned. Moon of Wales, your loveliness prevails.' Both poems – Solomon's and Huw's – are . . . lovely; one observes yet again that the literary tradition of David and Dafydd are not separate entities. Simply, the older tradition permeates the younger, there is a dialectic, a development. A seepage!

Raymond Garlick and Roland Mathias suggest that one piece typical of Welsh-flavoured praise poetry is George Herbert's sonnet, 'Prayer'; that it owns, moreover, 'characteristic devices of bardic craft: compound words and the heaping up of comparisons.' Not long before the publication of their Anglo-Welsh anthology, in short well before I read their introduction, it so happened that I wrote a sonnet based on Herbert's poem which I called 'Music'. It, too, consists of consecutive poetic definitions – though not of prayer but of music. Since both are brief I shall read them to you. First, 'Prayer':

Prayer

Prayer, the Church's banquet, Angel's age,
   God's breath in man returning to his birth,
   The soul in paraphrase, heart in pilgrimage,
The Christian plummet sounding heaven and earth;

Engine against th'Almighty, sinner's tower,
   Reversed thunder, Christ-side-piercing spear,
   The six days' world-transposing in an hour,
A kind of tune, which all things hear and fear;

Softness, and peace, and joy, and love, and bliss,
   Exalted Manna, gladness of the best,
   Heaven in ordinary, men well drest,
The Milky Way, the bird of Paradise,

   Church-bells beyond the stars heard, the soul's blood,
   The land of spices, something understood.

Now (excuse the impudence of following George Herbert) my own sonnet, 'Music':

Music

Music in the beginning. Before the word,
    voyaging of the spheres, their falling transport.
Like phoenix utterance, what Pythagoras heard;
    first hallucinogen, ritual's afterthought.

A place on no map. Hubbub behind high walls
    of Heaven – its bugged secrets filtering out:
numinous hauntings; sacerdotal mating-calls;
    decorous deliriums; an angel's shout.

If God's propaganda, then Devil's disgust,
    plainchant or symphony, carol or fugue;
King Saul's solace, St Cecilia's drug;
    silence's hiding place – like sunbeams' dust.

Sorrow's aggrandisements more plangent than sweet;
    the soul made audible, Time's other beat.

The question I would like to ask you here is what amalgam of influences are apparent in 'Music'? Because of its covert praise-component, its strategy of using a catalogue of analogues, should it be classed as an Anglo-Welsh poem? Is it of the tradition of David and Dafydd? Or, simply, is its influence only that of George Herbert himself?

II

When I was a schoolboy, my elder brothers Wilfred and Leo were already in their twenties, young adults. They became the most important influences in the direction of my life. Wilfred, when he himself became a doctor, newly qualified at the Welsh National School of Medicine here in Cardiff, came home one day to find me uselessly pushing a saucer of milk towards our sick cat, Merlin. I was a fourteen-year-old who wanted to play football for Cardiff City, rugby for Wales, cricket for Glamorgan.

'Better to become a doctor,' Wilfred suggested. 'I could pu'

your name down for the new Westminster Hospital they're plan-
ning in London.'

'I wouldn't mind being a vet,' I said, looking at the cat.

I did not fancy shifting to London. I resented even moving the
one and a half miles from Sandringham Road, Roath, Cardiff,
to Windermere Avenue, Penylan, Cardiff, as we were to do the
following year. For God's sake, who wanted to travel 160 miles
every Saturday to reach Ninian Park or Cardiff Arms Park? And
where, in London, would you get a better chip shop than the one
opposite the Globe Cinema?

By the time we moved to Windermere Avenue, Wilfred, with
my father approving, had responsibly charted my future. He
persuaded my parents to put my name down for Westminster
Hospital and, at school, I now turned to the science subjects –
physics, chemistry and biology – with a more purposeful interest.

If Wilfred set me towards studying Medicine, my brother Leo,
inadvertently, faced me towards Poetry. At school, at St Illtyd's
where I was taught by Christian Brothers, I did not enjoy our
poetry classes. It was, I thought, cissy stuff. Daffodils, Lesser
Celandines Skylarks, Cuckoos, Jug-jug, pu-we, to-witta-woo!
That sort of thing did not seem of moment. There was a war
going on in Spain; one of Leo's friends, Sid Hamm, had been
killed out there fighting for the International Brigade; Mussolini
was puffed out and ranting in Italy; Hitler, eyes thyrotoxic,
dangerously maniacal in Germany. There was sloth and unem-
ployment and depression in the Welsh valleys and the Prince of
Wales had said poshly, uselessly, 'Something must be done.' But
nothing was done, so what relevance, 'Cuckoo, jug-jug, pu-we,
to-witta-woo'?

At school we still sang, 'Let the prayer re-echo, God bless the
Prince of Wales,' though I mistakenly believed that patriotic lyric
to be 'Let the prairie echo, God bless the Prince of Wales', and
wondered vaguely where the devil those grass-waving prairies
were in mountainous Wales. At home, though, I read those left-
wing magazines Leo brought back and, in them, I discovered
poems of a political nature and of the war in Spain. How moved
I was, for instance, when I happened on 'Huesca', that simple,
direct poem by John Cornford. Not twenty-one, John Cornford
had been killed at the battle of Huesca while fighting for the
International Brigade. How poignant his melancholy premonition

of his own death; how terrible those lines of his, the last lines he ever wrote.

Poetry moved into the centre of my preoccupations gradually and that movement only truly commenced after I had read, in 1940, an anthology, *Poems for Spain*, edited by Stephen Spender. Here I encountered poets whose adult moral concerns and protestations engaged my own schoolboy wrath and indignation. Their voices had a passionate immediacy and their language was fresh, of the twentieth century. The raw, political poems of the Spanish peasant poet, Miguel Hernandez, especially, triggered me to try and express my own indignation about the horrors of the Spanish war in verse. Yes, naively, wanting to make political statements, I had begun to write verse voluntarily, not as an exercise for school. I showed my efforts to my elder brothers, and Wilfred, particularly, encouraged me.

The war in Spain ended and Hitler was screaming and given thunderous applause. It was not long before we heard our Prime Minister, Neville Chamberlain, utter on the BBC, 'I have to tell you that no understanding has been received and that consequently this country is at war with Germany.' My sister had married, had already left home. In 1940 it was Leo's turn to leave Wales. He was called up for the RAF. Later, Wilfred joined the Army. Suddenly the house seemed larger. There was only father, mother, me and the dog.

Perhaps it was fortunate for me that my brothers had to go away at this crucial period: at least it allowed me to develop unimpeded in my own tentative way – dreaming most of the time or browsing in Cardiff Central Library, or listening to Duke Ellington records or to the war news of the BBC, or playing games, or fumbling after girls, or preparing myself for a medical education, or writing a collocation of words that I wrongly called a poem.

III

Medical students, in their pre-clinical years, are allowed long summer vacations. In Cardiff, I spent much of my holidays in the Central Library reading poetry. First I reached for the books on the left-hand side top shelf of the Twentieth Century Poetry

Section: Richard Aldington, W. H. Auden. Then I worked my way across and downward. I read for pleasure, in this untutored way, alphabetically, not chronologically, without benefit of knowing who was considered by critics to be worthy, who to be scorned! One day I asked a girl called Joyce Herbert who was reading English at Cardiff's University College if she had heard of Dylan Thomas. My question provoked a little chuckle and a contemptuous, 'Of course.'

Dylan Thomas's poems powerfully engaged me – too much so, for a number of my own poems which can be discovered in my first volume, *After Every Green Thing*, are touched by his manner. Certain phrases sound like Dylan's cast-offs: 'harp of sabbaths', 'choir of wounds'. Admiring his work as I did, naturally I became curious about the man who lived not far away from my own home-patch. I was most intrigued when Leo, soon after he was demobbed from the RAF, told me that he had met my hero and that, moreover, Dylan Thomas had related to him a remarkable dream.

It seemed that Dylan, in this dream, entered a huge cavern or chamber in which he witnessed a biblical scene being enacted: Job, head bowed in grief, sat on the ground, crosslegged, with his three bearded comforters in silent attendance. Dylan quit this chamber to enter another and here saw Absalom, caught by his long hair, struggling and swinging from the boughs of a great oak. Then the dreamer entered another chamber where frenzied crowds danced around a golden calf. He passed from chamber to chamber, cavern leading into cavern, going back in time, watching Jacob wrestling with the angel or Abraham, in rage, destroying the wooden idols. At last, Dylan came to the ultimate chamber. He entered into almost darkness. He peered. Something was glinting against the rock of the back wall. He approached. Two skeletons became visible: the skeletons of a man and a woman, hand in hand.

That dream was surely a waking vision, rather than one recalled from sleep, and perhaps it owed something to William Blake's memorable fancies in 'The Marriage of Heaven and Hell'? No matter, Leo's recounting of it made me pause and wonder. I relished it and, soon enough, back in London, retold it to literary friends in one of the cafés of Swiss Cottage that, in those post-war years, I regularly visited.

I had lodgings in Swiss Cottage. It was a cosmopolitan area with a remarkably vivid café life because of the refugees, mostly Jews, from Austria and Germany. They had settled in the district. So ubiquitous were they that the bus conductors, approaching Swiss Cottage, would bang the bell and shout out, 'Next stop, Tel Aviv.' In cafés such as The Cosmo or The Cordial, loitered theatre and film people such as Peter Berg, Lotte Lenya, Peter Zadek; or writers like Elias Canetti (who insisted on being called Canetti since he loathed his first name), the poet Erich Fried (who happened to have an abnormally thick-boned skull and could thump it, bang bang bang, against a wall for our amusement) and Rudi Nassauer (who had been influenced by Dylan Thomas even more than I had so that he thundered out his poems in an arresting but unnatural booming voice that would have delighted Dylan Thomas's elocution teacher).

In this ambience I heard of European poets who had hardly featured in the Poetry Section of Cardiff's Central Library. I read some of these in translation and one, especially, became a passion with me: Rainer Maria Rilke. How exciting to read such praise-poetry lines as:

> There is nothing too small but my tenderness paints
> it large on a background of gold.

When I read Rilke's *Letters to a Young Poet* I felt he addressed not merely Herr Kappus but me: 'This before all: ask yourself in the quietest hour of your night: *must* I write? Dig down into yourself for a deep answer. And if this should be in the affirmative, if you may meet this solemn question with a strong and simple, *I must*, then build your life according to this necessity. . . .' I responded, of course, with a strenuous, 'I must' and I have, though it may sound somewhat grand to say so, unconsciously as much as consciously, ordered my life ever since to allow for this central need.

The eighth letter addressed to Kappus from Sweden in 1904 stimulated me to write a poem called 'The Uninvited'. It is the only poem I am now willing to acknowledge that appeared in my first volume, *After Every Green Thing*. Rilke, in that letter, spoke of how certain sorrowful experiences alter us because of what they may engender. When we are open to important moments of sorrow, argued Rilke, then our future 'sets foot in us'. Though we could easily believe nothing has truly happened, our destiny begins and 'we have been changed as a house is changed into which a guest has entered'.

Rilke's influence endured and could set me ticking like a wheel of a bicycle going downhill. In 1954 I wrote a number of poems on existentialist themes, among them 'Duality' and 'The Trial' as a result of reading a passage in *The Notebook of Malte Laurids Brigge*. Here Rilke described an encounter with a woman who was deep in thought, completely sunk into herself, her head in her hands. 'At the corner of the Rue Notre-Dame-des-Champs,' wrote Rilke, 'I began to walk softly as soon as I saw her. . . . The street was too empty; its emptiness was bored with itself; it caught my step from under my feet and clattered about with it hither and yon, as with a wooden clog. The woman took fright and was torn too quickly out of herself, too violently, so that her face remained in her two hands. I could see it lying in them, its hollow form. It cost me an indescribable effort to keep my eyes on those hands and not to look at what had been torn out of them. I shuddered to see a face thus from the inside, but I was still more afraid of the naked, flayed, head without a face.'

Rilke not only triggered me to write a number of poems but taught me lessons which I took to heart. In his first letter to Kappus, for instance, he averred, 'A work of art is good if it has grown out of necessity.' I assented to that: so many poems that I admired most had sprung from the stress of a personal predicament or from an active emotion like indignation or rage or love. Had I not been turned on originally to poetry because of the urgent cries of help from some poets in beleaguered Spain – poets like Miguel Hernandez? Had I not been moved by John Cornford's 'Huesca' – or going back through the centuries by John Clare's 'I am' and William Cowper's 'The Castaway'?

Again Rilke suggested that one should be committed to difficulty. 'We know little,' he wrote, 'but that we must hold to the difficult. . . .' Poetry, true crafted poetry was scandalously difficult to write. And the practice of medicine, too, at least for me, was hardly an easy ride.

Some poems of Rilke, too, became guru-lessons for me. At a hospital bedside, in a consulting room, I have listened, as a doctor must, purely to patients – never having to silence the clamour that my own senses might make. But discarding the white coat, encountering strangers of interest, I have tended to talk too much, to display, rather than to listen. Then I have reminded myself of these lines by Rilke that I know, in Babette Deutsch's translation, by heart:

> If only there were stillness, full, complete.
> If all the random and approximate
> were muted, with neighbours' laughter, for your sake,
> and if the clamour that my senses make
> did not confound the vigil I would keep –
>
> Then in a thousandfold thought I could think
> you out, even to your utmost brink
> and (while a smile endures) possess you, giving
> you away, as though I were but giving thanks
> to all the living.

There are those who cannot bear Rilke – among them friends of mine, poets, whose opinion I generally value; and indeed there are many occasions when Rilke, in his letters seems too sanctimonious, too high flown, phoney even. I thought this when I first read him. In the margins of my old copy of *Letters to a Young Poet*, years ago, I scrawled, 'Note here his evident insincerity.' Or I remarked on his patronising attitudes and pomposity. I argued in an abbreviated form (with question marks and exclamation marks) against the poetic ideas he proposed about such matters as the attainment of inner solitude, of the need to be alone as one was in childhood when surrounding adults seemed so busy and distant. Yet arguments with a mentor can be valuable in themselves, be productive. I disliked then, as most Welshmen would, the way Rilke, encountering others, thrust out his arm, as it were, to keep them away; his need to distance other people as if other people were vulgarly dangerous. Years later I wrote a poem concerning a lady with these Rilkean attitudes. If the poem that follows, 'Close Up' (NB no hyphen) is any good at all then my argument with Rilke was not entirely worthless:

> Often you seem to be listening to a music
> that others cannot hear. Rilke would have loved you:
> you never intrude, you never ask questions
> of those, crying in the dark, who are most near.

You always keep something of yourself to yourself
in the electric bars, even in bedrooms.
Rilke would have praised you: your nearness is far,
and, therefore, your distance like the very stars.

Yet some things you miss and some things you lose
by keeping your arm outstretched; and some things
you'll never know unless one, at least, knows you
like a close-up, in detail – blow by human blow.

What I could have learnt and should have learnt from Rilke
was the value of experiences in making a poem. That I was to
learn later when I began to believe poems should not begin with
ideas but rather spring from true or imagined experience. One
poet whom I met in Swiss Cottage, Denise Levertov, was more
percipient than me about this. She has said in *Light Up the Cave*
that her first lesson from Rilke was to experience *what you live*.
I should have heeded, right from the beginning, how Rilke told
the secret that verses amount to little when one begins to write
them when young. Rilke continues, 'One ought to wait and gather
sense and sweetness, a whole life long, and a long life if possible,
and then, quite at the end, one might perhaps be able to write
ten good lines. For verses are not, as people imagine, simply
feelings (we have these soon enough); they are experiences. In
order to write a single verse, one must see many cities, and men
and things; . . . One must be able to return in thought to roads
in unknown regions, to unexpected encounters, and to partings
that had been long foreseen; to days of childhood that are still
indistinct . . . to days spent in rooms withdrawn and quiet, and
to mornings by the sea, to the sea itself, to oceans, to nights of
travel that rushed along loftily and flew with all the stars – and
still it is not enough to be able to think of all this. There must
be memories of many nights of love, each one unlike the others,
of the screams of women in labour, and of women in childbed,
light and blanched and sleeping, shutting themselves in. But one
must also have been beside the dying, must have sat beside the
dead in a room with open windows and with fitful noises. And
still it is not enough yet to have memories. One must be able to
forget them when they are many, and one must have the immense
patience to wait until they come again. For it is the memories
themselves that matter. Only when they have turned to blood

within us, to glance and gesture, nameless and no longer to be distinguished from ourselves – only then can it happen that in a most rare hour the first word of a poem arises in their midst and goes forth from them.'

IV

In the structuring of experience into poems I have sometimes drawn on literary texts in a way that I suspect is not visible or audible to others. The texts are generally soluble in the poems. Sometimes they are not soluble and could be discerned if the reader happened on certain sources. For instance, I have, in recent years, drawn on brief Talmudic or Midrashic lesson-stories. Here is one example: Rabbi Eliezer was sick. Rabbi Yohanan came to visit him. He saw Rabbi Eliezer lying in a dark house. Rabbi Yohanan bared his arm and the room lit up. He saw that Rabbi Eliezer was crying. He said to him, 'Why are you crying? Is it for the Torah in which you have not studied enough? We have learned, do more, do less, it matters not, as long as one's heart is turned to heaven. . . .' Rabbi Eliezer replied, 'I am crying over this beauty of yours which one day will wither in the dust.' Rabbi Yohanan said, 'You are right to cry over that.' And they wept together.

Under the influence of that succinct anecdote I wrote a narrative poem called 'The Silence of Tudor Evans'. I'll repeat the title because it makes an important point: 'The Silence of Tudor Evans'. It goes like this:

> Gwen Evans, singer and trainer of singers,
>   who, in 1941, warbled
> an encore (Trees) at Porthcawl Pavilion,
>   lay in bed, not ½ her weight and dying.
> Her husband, Tudor, drew the noise of curtains.
>
> Then, in the artificial dark, she whispered,
>   'Please send for Professor Mandlebaum.'
> She raised her head pleadingly from the pillow,
>   her horror-movie eyes thyrotoxic.
> 'Who?' Tudor asked, remembering, remembering.
>
> Not Mandlebaum, not that renowned professor

whom Gwen had once met on holiday;
not that lithe ex-Wimbledon tennis player
   and author of *Mediastinal Tumours*;
not that swine Mandlebaum of 1941?

Mandlebaum doodled in his hotel bedroom.
   For years he had been in speechless sloth.
But now for Gwen and old times' sake he, first-class,
   alert, left echoing Paddington for
a darkened sickroom and two large searching eyes.

She sobbed when he gently took her hand in his.
   'But my dear, why are you crying?'
Because, Max, you're quite unrecognisable.'
   'I can't scold you for crying about that,'
said Mandlebaum and he, too, began to weep.

They wept together (and Tudor closed his eyes)
   Gwen, singer and trainer of singers
because she was dying; and he, Mandlebaum,
   ex-physician and ex-tennis player,
because he had become so ugly and so old.

I have plundered different Midrashic texts to energise other poems, not a few of which have been portrait poems, a genre that has been favoured, according to Garlick and Mathias, for centuries because of 'Welsh curiosity about other people.' To be sure, there are no kept secrets in Wales. All women leak; all men are moles. Everybody knows Dai, the spy. Or to put it more diplomatically: we gossip so much because we are all so interested in the unfathomable strangeness of other human beings.

If what Garlick and Mathias say about portrait-poems is true, then it would seem that in an odd way I may have inadvertently once again tried to make the traditions of David and Dafydd confluent.

V

In February 1961, I became involved with the astonishing Poetry and Jazz concerts that were to take place with regular success in the theatres, town halls, school halls and public libraries of Britain during the rest of the decade. I had received a phone call from a young man called Jeremy Robson inviting me to read at the Hampstead Town Hall along with Jon Silkin and Lydia Slater who would recite her brother's poems in translation. (Lydia Slater was the sister of Boris Pasternak). Jeremy Robson did not inform me that he planned intervals of jazz between the poets' readings nor that he, himself, would read his own poetry especially written for jazz accompaniment. In addition, he omitted to tell me that the comedian of Goon fame, Spike Milligan, would also feature.

I was, I suppose, a literary snob! If I had known the 'pop' nature of the Hampstead Town Hall reading, if I had seen the advertisements, I doubt whether I would have accepted Jeremy Robson's invitation. I set out that evening expecting to participate in a genteel poetry-reading with the usual numbers attending and, thus, I was baffled to discover, at the doors of the Town Hall, a huge crowd demanding entrance while a distraught porter shouted, 'Full up, Full up.' I had difficulty, in fact, in pushing my way through. Inside, hundreds sat on the Town Hall's upright wooden chairs, others sprawled in the aisles, leant on the side walls and back walls while jazz negligently blared. Soon Spike Milligan appeared in dramatic spotlight saying, 'I thought I'd begin with a sonnet by Shakespeare but then I thought why should I? He never reads any of mine.' The concert was not solemn.

Over the next six years Jeremy Robson organized hundreds more of these concerts, inviting a score or so of alternating, different poets to take part. Some, such as Vernon Scannell, John Smith, Jeremy Robson himself, read their poems to jazz; others such as Ted Hughes, Laurie Lee and myself, read our poems 'straight', unaccompanied, believing as we did that each poem had its own music and, for that matter, its own silences. (Stevie Smith sometimes *sang* her poems in a peculiarly flat voice.) The enthusiastic, large audiences clapped frequently and seemed to be genuinely entertained. Later they bought books (in the interval) to investigate in private, on the page, the poems they had heard publicly in the auditorium.

We always arrived in one or another provincial town at lighting-up time. I still feel that on entering such places as Nottingham or Leicester somehow the lamp posts should all jerk into life, and on quitting them the hands of the clock should turn fast and turn again until the streets are late, deserted, the shops darkened except for the one, lonely, lit Indian restaurant that beckons jazz musicians and poets to eat and unwind.

Over the next six years, did the regular practice of reading poems aloud to large audiences affect, consciously or unconsciously, our strategy in structuring poems? When Dylan Thomas began to read to proliferating mass audiences the idioplasm of his poetry gradually altered. His poems, while growing more complex in their rhythmic orchestration, also became somewhat less dense, less recondite generally. There were seductive dangers in being exposed to large audiences and I daresay some poets sometimes succumbed to them and not in the way Dylan Thomas did. In my case, I know that my poems about this time became more conversationally pitched but I doubt if this was the result of performance and live audience. When I wrote a poem I did not usually consider reader or listener. The exception to that was in writing longer poems. Then, at a certain point in their maturation, I would become aware that I would actually enjoy reading this or that one out loud to receive a public response. When I wrote plays I had to be aware of audience, of allowing the narrative its tensions and relaxations. So, too, with a long poem which otherwise could freeze an audience into lassitude. In writing, for instance, 'The Smile Was', about 1965, after some drafts I knew I would read it out loud at a Poetry and Jazz concert. I became more aware of the problems of pace, density and humour than might otherwise have been the case. And I ensured that the rhythms did not become too monotonous, that the repetitions of sound patterns were appropriately varied. Once Eliot had generously said of a play of mine that it had the virtue of being both for the stage and the study. I would like to think some of my longer poems could be similarly characterized.

VI

Most of us hardly question what influences us and do not observe our barely fathomable metamorphosis steadily. We merely mark how our life situation may have changed or how our interests have been developed: how our children have grown up, how others we loved became much older or died. All authors, though, have visible concrete evidence of their own internal changes: they can turn to their artefacts – in my case, to my plays as well as to my poems – and see how these give witness to altering attitudes, preoccupations, arguments with oneself. They recall debts to other writers, textual influences, transient or repetitive experiences and moods, successes and failures, occasions and relationships. Poems on the page lie there and do not lie: their own progenitor can scrutinize them as if they were spiritual X-rays.

Certainly my poems relate, in hidden narrative, my true biography. There is hardly an important occasion in my life that is not covertly profiled or overtly re-inhabited in my poems. So when I open my *Collected Poems* and turn, say, to page 107, I suffer almost an abreaction as I hold again my father's hand while he is dying in Llandough Hospital in 1964; or when the book falls open on page 131 I can remember, altogether less painfully, how with my wife and children, I attended a demonstration in Trafalgar Square, in 1968, against the war in Vietnam.

Poems can remind me of such things because they are rooted in my mental life, in my experiences, some mundane, some dramatic. I recall the words of Rilke again: 'In order to write a single verse one must be able to return in thought . . . to unexpected encounters . . . to days of childhood that are still indistinct . . . to nights of love. . . . But one must also have been beside the dying, must have sat beside the dead in a room with open windows and with fitful noises.' I have experienced such things as so many others have; and I have done my best to tell of these things in the best way I can, with what gift I have, sometimes going to other men's texts like a sleepwalker and sometimes wide awake.

Nor have I worried about such matters, for I agree with Goethe when he remarked. . . 'We are all collective beings, let us place ourselves as we may. For how little *have* we, and *are* we, that we can strictly call our own property? We must all receive and learn both from those who were before us, and from those who are with us. Even the greatest genius would not go far if he tried to owe everything to his own internal self. But many very good men do not comprehend that; and they grope in darkness for half a life, with their dreams of originality. I have known artists who boasted of having followed no master, and of having to thank their own genius for everything. Fools! as if that were possible at all; and as if the world would not force itself upon them at every step, and make something of them in spite of their own stupidity. . . . And, indeed, what is there good in us, if it is not the power and the inclination to appropriate to ourselves the resources of the outward world, and to make them subservient to our higher ends. . . . The main point is to have a great will, and skill and perseverance to carry it out.'

And here's the curious thing: after decades of writing poems, every poet, I believe, if he takes his own work seriously as he should, comes under the influence of it. When a poet begins to write a poem there is no reader; but as he concludes his poem he himself becomes the first reader. Sometimes the last! He receives his own words. Thereafter, in subtle ways, his poems even as they may recede for others, remain for him strangely active. They help to determine not only how he will write but how he will live. Some may argue that poetry is a useless thing. It influences no one. But whatever else poems do, or do not do, they profoundly alter the man or the woman who wrote them.

Appendix 3
THE CHAIRMAN

Those who pronounce your name wrongly: 'We are pleased to welcome you 'ere tonight, Mr Abs.' Those whose welcome seems over-profuse, flatulent, as when I arrived for the Cambridge Festival of 1983. 'Oh, I'm so glad *you've* arrived. He's arrived. Oh wonderful. Dannie Abse's arrived. We're all so pleased, so pleased to see you. Wonderful. You see, there's a Greek poet here scheduled to read tomorrow and he desperately needs a doctor to write him a prescription.'

Those whose introductions are long and tedious, or just untrue: 'Mr Abse is not only a poet but also a Member of Parliament.' Those who alienate the neutral audience with killing overpraise – that time in Kent when the chairman's eulogy concluded with – 'And, *in addition*, Dr Abse's the greatest British comic poet since Chaucer!' I felt then I should be funny, render the now melancholy-eyed audience (they resembled mourners at a funeral) 'seismic with laughter' by emulating, perhaps, Spike Milligan: 'I thought I'd start, as a matter of fact, by reading you some of Chaucer; but then I decided, the hell with that, why should I? He never reads any of mine.'

Less rare are those chairmen who prove to be not merely inept but plainly malignant. Mr Norman Moore, for instance, who officiated – that is the correct word – at a reading I gave in the Lake District, one summer's evening in 1981. Not long before that occasion I had, perhaps foolishly, contributed to a series of articles in *Punch* called 'Success'. When Alan Coren commissioned me to write that piece perhaps I should have quoted Chekhov: 'Success? Write about my success? What's the

162

criterion for success? You need to be God to distinguish success from failure unerringly. I'm off to a dance.' But how was I to know that Mr Norman Moore was later to pick up that copy of *Punch* in his dentist's waiting room?

When I was called for at the hotel and taken to the poetry-reading venue the nice blonde driver said, 'I'm worried about the chairman for tonight. You see Bill who wrote to you had to go into hospital to have his appendix out. It was an emergency – and they've asked Norman Moore to substitute.'

'Norman Moore?'

'He knows nothing about poetry. But he's the local panjandrum, a Tory councillor, and used to acting as chairman. I suppose it will be all right.'

In the hall I was introduced to Mr Moore, a tall man, tall as a publisher. He was talking to some of the audience and my blonde friend interrupted him in mid-flow. He was not *homey*. He did not even offer me a glacial hand. He hardly nodded before turning back to his admirers. Five minutes later, before we went together on to the slightly raised platform, he did deign to address me briefly. 'I take it you'll be through in an hour. I have a later appointment.' Someone once said that there is no one so pompous as a local celebrity. Norman Moore was obviously one helluva local celebrity but I felt no antagonism nor did I expect him, of course, to harbour any ill-feelings towards me.

Soon he rose to address the audience. About eighty men and women draped the wooden chairs, having come to this focal point from different parts of the Lake District. 'I have never read a book by Dr Abse,' Mr Moore commenced, 'but recently I came across a piece he wrote in *Punch*, a magazine I might add that does not usually come my way. In *Punch* it says, ha ha ha, that he's a success.'

I glanced towards him surprised by the acidulous tone of his voice. 'A success!' he jeered loudly. 'Moreover it appears he has two elder brothers, one called Wilfred, a psychoanalyst, an *eminent* psychoanalyst, it says in *Punch*. Ha!'

The audience, I sensed, had become nervously alert. This was not going to be a conventional introduction.

'We've had a *psy-cho-analyst* living round here,' Mr Moore boomed as loud as nitro-glycerine, 'and now he's gone to New Mexico for good. Ha! And ... are ... we ... all ... *glad*.'

The audience, unsmiling, silent on their wooden chairs, looked shifty as Norman Moore continued, assuming the role of prosecuting counsel in a murder case. 'Moreover in *Punch* – hmmm! – it says he has a second brother, one Leo Abse, an MP., A *Labour* MP. Why, we've heard of *his* activities. I tell you if he came here and put up for election he'd come *last*. After the Communist!'

At this point I felt obliged to interrupt mildly with, 'Thank you for your kind introduction.' I looked towards the jury, I mean the audience, for support and somebody in the back did titter. But our homomorph of a chairman thundered on. 'To be frank I have read *one* of Dr Abse's poems and I tell you *it is blasphemous*.'

As he continued with his bizarre invective I thought what the hell am I doing here, a sitting target. I thought I may as well go home, but home was hundreds of miles away; besides, many of the audience, too, had travelled some distance. Mr Moore was now gently pointing out that I was a *medical* doctor and how *medical* doctors these days were responsible for so many iatrogenic diseases. He was not trying to be funny and by the time he sat down I felt too full of arrows, too bruised to be witty about his lengthy, abusive introduction.

Instead, I found myself on my feet remarking seriously that, yes, I did have two elder brothers and yes I was fond of them both, both valuable citizens and yes as a matter of fact I was proud of them etc. Then I began my poetry reading.

I have never encountered an audience so sympathetic. Thanks to Mr Norman Moore's rousing introduction they laughed at all my tired jokes, applauded poems loudly, and listened to my every word as if I were, if not the messiah come, at least poor old St Sebastian, bloody and heroic.